Grief and Loss

Theories and Skills for Helping Professionals

Katherine Walsh-Burke

Springfield College

PEARSON

Boston • New York • San Francisco
Mexico City • Montreal • Toronto • London • Madrid • Munich • Paris
Hong Kong • Singapore • Tokyo • Cape Town • Sydney

Series Editor: Patricia Quinlin
Editorial Assistant: Sara Holliday
Marketing Manager: Kris Ellis-Levy
Production Editor: Greg Erb
Composition and Prepress Buyer: Linda Cox
Manufacturing Buyer: JoAnne Sweeney
Electronic Composition: Publishers' Design and Production Services, Inc.
Cover Administrator: Kristina Mose-Libon

For related titles and support materials, visit our online catalog at www.ablongman.com.

Library of Congress Cataloging-in-Publication Data

Walsh-Burke, Katherine.
    Grief and loss : theories and skills for helping professionals / Katherine Walsh-Burke.— 1st ed.
        p. cm.
    Includes bibliographical references and index.
    ISBN 0-205-39881-2 (pbk.)
    1. Loss (Psychology) 2. Grief. 3. Counseling. I. Title.

BF724.3.L66W35 2005
155.9'37—dc22   20040066184

Printed in the United States of America

10 9 8 7 6 5 4 3 2 1   10 09 08 07 06 05

Contents

8 *Self-Care: Sustaining Hope, Helpfulness, and Competence in Working with Grief* **94**

Preface

The journey of a thousand miles begins with the first step.

—Chinese Proverb

Why do human service professionals and educators need the information this book provides?

Most of us who have chosen to help others through a professional career have done so because we wanted to help others improve or maintain their health and well-being, increase their knowledge and skills, and to enhance their quality of life. Few of us chose our careers as a path to helping people grieve. I certainly did not. As a 22-year-old recent college grad, I entered a graduate training program in social work thinking I would like to help children and families make the most of their education through school-based interventions. My first internship was in an inner city elementary school in the south Bronx in 1975. At that time, the burned-out buildings surrounding Public School 141 were evidence of the invasion of drugs and urban decay that were taking the lives and hope of many families in the neighborhood. The children and parents on my caseload revealed to me the daily losses they endured through violence, illness, injury, and poverty, and I came to understand that many of their struggles in school were connected to these losses. Thus my education in grief and loss began. Part of this education, as challenging as it has been, has also involved becoming aware of the strengths in those who experience loss and the rewards of supporting them through the grieving process.

Over the past twenty-nine years, continued interactions with students and professionals in many different disciplines have taught me that inevitably every professional helper will be called upon—some more frequently than others—to work with individuals, families, groups, and communities who are experiencing loss and the grief that accompanies it. This book is designed to provide you with core knowledge and skills that will prepare you to do this more effectively.

Why have I written this book?

Imagine the following scenarios:

- A nutritionist monitoring a middle-aged man in a dialysis center finds the man is struggling to comply with his dialysis regimen and dietary restrictions. When the nutritionist asks him what is making it difficult he expresses a torrent of anger at the loss of his ability to carry on with his work as a traveling sales manager.
- A special education teacher meets with the parents of a child who has recently been diagnosed with a reading disability. The mother begins to cry during the meeting, acknowledging her sadness, while the father vents his anger at the delay in the diagnosis.
- A nurse in a VA Hospital neurology unit is asked, by the wife of a veteran who has just been diagnosed with a life-limiting neurological disease, for a referral for grief counseling for herself and her teenaged children.
- A radiation technologist observes the husband of a patient sitting in tears in the waiting room as his wife undergoes a diagnostic procedure following the discovery of a breast lump.
- A college soccer coach faces his distraught team following a tragic automobile accident in which their star player has died.
- The physical, occupational and speech therapy team members working with their elderly patient find it difficult to engage him in his rehabilitation program following a car accident in which he and his wife sustained life-threatening injuries.
- A school principal receives calls from parents and school board members asking for advice after the unexpected death of a beloved school secretary.
- A human resources specialist in a large corporation meets with an employee to discuss changes in family health care coverage and other benefits. During the meeting the employee begins to cry about the divorce that has prompted these changes.
- A physician's assistant in a busy OBGYN practice encounters unexpected anger in her patient during a routine checkup in which there are no unusual findings. The patient was hoping to be pregnant for a second time and is angry and frustrated with the secondary infertility she is experiencing and perceives this as a loss.

Each of these scenarios is an actual situation that I have been consulted about by one of my students or a professional colleague. Many more of the examples in this book are drawn from my own practice as a social worker in a variety of settings. In a VA Hospital neurology unit and then in a rehabilitation facility, my role as a social worker involved helping families adjust to chronic illnesses and injuries. As a clinical social worker at a comprehensive cancer center, my role on the interdisciplinary team was primarily to provide counseling to individuals diagnosed with cancer, but I also led support groups for the staff to help relieve the stress of this intense work.

Later, as a director of psychosocial services in a community hospice program, it was my responsibility to design bereavement programs and provide education and support to our staff as well as teachers, camp counselors, and community organizations coping with loss. Yet, the inspiration for this text came from my experiences teaching at Springfield College, a small liberal arts college in New England. In the spring semester of 2002, I was consulted by several departments, including my own, to provide guidance to students and faculty who were grieving unanticipated losses. First, a faculty member in the neighboring school of allied health was diagnosed with life-limiting cancer and died. This loss left students in shock and created a vast void in the small department. I was asked to appear as a guest lecturer on the topic of grief, which was usually taught by the department's faculty. But these instructors were struggling to cope with their own grief and therefore asked for assistance. The physical therapy students I met with were able to identify a wide array of situations they encountered in their work related to loss, and we used their own reactions to the loss of their mentor to discuss the mix of grief reactions they encountered in their clients.

Two months later, students in a number of departments within the college were affected by another death in the college community. A respected guidance counselor in a city high school died during a classroom altercation with one of his troubled students. Interns from our college's education department and the School of Social Work were carrying out their internships in this high school and had worked closely with the counselor. Shocked and saddened by this tragic death themselves, they sought my guidance in how to help the students and faculty of this and other city schools who were angry, frightened and emotionally distraught.

Then, only weeks before the close of the semester, our School of Social Work experienced the death of one of our own students. Just married and about to graduate with her MSW degree, Mary, a third-year student, died in an automobile accident. I had served as her advisor and initially felt overwhelmed with my own grief. Yet, there were other students' needs to consider, as well as the needs of her family and those of the fragile clients with whom she had worked in her field practicum at a therapeutic group home. Working with an ad hoc committee of students and faculty, our school community was able to respond to effectively address all of these needs.

These experiences and subsequent conversations and collaborations with colleagues in the fields of rehabilitation, education, corrections, and human services highlighted the fact that all of us, as professionals, need to be prepared to help our clients, colleagues, and organizations, as well as ourselves, with the inevitable losses and the impact of grief that we will encounter in our work. Many of the examples in this book were written by students working in very diverse settings who have taken a course in loss and grief that is typically oversubscribed each year in our program. Their comments perhaps best describe why professionals need to learn about loss and grief.

"I feel that studying this topic has given me the tools and understanding to work effectively with people who are either dying or losing someone they care about. The initial questions pertaining to loss put me in touch with feelings I had thought were long buried, and also made me realize the importance of beginning the work to resolve them."

"This class has reminded me to get the care I need to be an effective helper. As Rando (1984) states, 'We must attend to our own needs for relief from these demands [of working closely with loss]; if we don't, we will hurt ourselves and diminish our capability to help others' (p. 443)."

"This class, although sad at times, really made me think about having things in order in my own life, and it taught me about the various ways of dealing with grieving people, on a professional as well as a personal level. In the past when someone died, I didn't know what to say. I've learned a lot and thought about unresolved grief, which I hadn't thought about in a very long time."

While students who study loss and grief consistently attest to the value of learning about this important topic, too few professional training programs and textbooks address the topic adequately. Even mental health training programs do not routinely include loss and grief in their content. "Grief issues, both death-related and non-death related, are concerns which clients may present to counselors. It would seem essential, therefore, that counselor preparation programs include training for grief counseling in the body and knowledge and range of skills which they offer to counselor trainees. In fact, very little has appeared in the literature regarding either the content or the method of teaching grief counseling in counselor preparation programs (Humphrey, 1993). This book is intended to provide students with essential theoretical concepts and practical guidelines related to grief. Though preparation and planning cannot alleviate the strong emotions related to loss that we, our clients and our colleagues, will experience, it can help us be more effective in managing the wide array of reactions and responses we will encounter. It is my hope that the contents of this book will help you as you endeavor to help others.

What is covered in this text?

This text discusses theory and skills to inform a broad range of professional helpers who inevitably work with people who are grieving a loss. Whether you are a teacher, a member of your employer's human resources department, a corrections or parole officer, a health care provider, or a child and family services professional, you will encounter children, teens, or adults coping with symbolic and actual losses. Sometimes rapid assessment and intervention are required, such as when an accident or unanticipated death occurs in a community or institution. At other times anticipatory grief, anniversary reactions, or unresolved losses impede a student's or employee's performance. Attuned helpers can provide immediate support and linkages to community resources in these situations. In some settings, such as health care facilities and senior centers, immediate losses involving patients, family members, or co-workers are common. In these settings, workers can provide support to each other as well as clients, and can help to identify those who may need specialized services.

In each of these situations, the following key areas of knowledge and skill are essential:

- Understanding normal and complicated grief reactions.
- Identifying actual as well as symbolic losses.
- Knowledge of the factors that positively and negatively influence grief reactions.
- Familiarity with resources and interventions that are effective in helping those who are grieving.

The text reviews clues to distinguish normal or expectable grief reactions from those that may require more expert intervention from a grief specialist. Factors such as life stage, culture, spirituality, gender, and community support systems that are known to influence grief reactions are addressed. Each chapter also includes exercises that will help to prepare you for this important aspect of your work. Web support to the text includes links to key resources from the Internet that enhance knowledge, address specialized skills, and provide downloadable brochures, reading lists, and other information to assist you in helping others. Some of these are included at the end of each chapter and additional resources can be found on the companion Web site for this text at www.ablongman.com. The appendixes include FAQ sheets, activities, and materials that you can duplicate and share with clients or colleagues. Together these components are designed to prepare you to be successful in your personal and professional helping endeavors.

One of the most beautiful compensations of this life is that no man can sincerely try to help another without helping himself.

—Ralph Waldo Emerson

References

Humphrey, K. (1993). Grief counseling training in counselor preparation programs in the United States: A preliminary report. *International Journal for the Advancement of Counseling*, 16, 333–340.

Rando, T. (1984). *Grief, dying and death: Clinical interventions for caregivers*. Champaign, IL: Research Press Company.

Acknowledgments

It is a snowy morning in January, the beginning of a new year. I have been blessed with the gift of a stay at my friends Mickey and Julie's retreat house in Vermont to complete the writing of this text. The falling snow makes everything appear peaceful. I begin my retreat by opening the door and embracing the view—a vast field, circled by gently sloping hills. Smoke curls from the chimney of a house in the distance. I breathe in the cold, refreshing air and call to mind the recent letters and phone calls I have received. One was from the mother of a teenager who died twenty years ago of leukemia, following a hard-fought battle. She has written every Christmas since I met them as a social worker at the Dana Farber Cancer Institute. This year she writes, "I still can't believe that David has been gone from us for so long. I think of him every day. His little nephews have heard all about him and know that his spirit is with us all. Dear Kathy, you were such a lifeline to us during our darkest hours. We love you and thank you still."

I also recall a phone message, left out of the blue from Dotti. I met her family when her 43-year-old husband was treated for cancer more than twenty years ago. Although we kept in touch for the first year after his death, I have not had contact with her since I moved from Boston to western Massachusetts eighteen years ago. Her message on my answering machine says, "I am moving and was going through my address book. I don't know if you remember me but you helped me in ways I will never forget, and I just wanted to call and tell you that, and to wish you and your family well." My daughters smile with a mixture of bemusement and concern at the tears that inevitably spring up when I receive these calls from families who have endured the most painful of losses. Then my daughters put their arms around me and reassure all of us with the words, "It's ok, mom. It means you helped."

And so this book is dedicated to my family—especially Lauren and Jessy, my parents, brother, and sisters—and my dear friends, and to all the families, students, friends, and colleagues who have helped me to live and learn. I hope that the content of this book will help others to risk and reap the rewards of helping others with grief and loss.

1

Loss Experiences That Generate Grief Reactions

> *Grief knits two hearts in closer bonds than happiness ever can; and common sufferings are far stronger links than common joys.*
>
> —Alphonse de Lamartine

Basic Facts about Loss and Grief

- Every year, two million people die in the United States of America.
- If each of these deaths affects just five other people, at least ten million people are affected each year.
- Chronic illnesses such as cancer, heart disease, and diabetes account for two of every three deaths. These illnesses create many losses before death is even anticipated.
- Accidents are the leading cause of death for children under age eighteen. Accidents are also the cause of many disabling injuries, creating loss of mobility, fine motor skills, and cognitive functions.
- In 1999, the most recent year for which statistics are published by the U.S. Dept. of Health and Human Services, 568,000 children were removed from their biological families to live in foster care. These children, their biological and foster parents, siblings, teachers, and social workers are all affected by loss and grief.

- According to predictions based on the U.S. census approximately 43 percent of marriages in the U.S. will end in divorce.
- Some parents and children who experience divorce consider adjusting to the losses associated with it to be as challenging as the losses associated with death.
- The tragic events of September 11, 2001 immediately affected people all over the world, and particularly in the U.S. The traumatic losses associated with these terrorist attacks, along with other tragedies such as the Columbine High School shootings, have an impact on individuals and communities far beyond what can currently be understood.

How many times have you heard the phrase "loss is a part of life"? Yet, have you thought about how loss will impact the work you have chosen to do or how you will respond when someone you are working with is grieving? If you are reading this text, you are most likely a student in training or already working with people. If so, you will be better prepared than many professionals to help those who are grieving.

Many professionals report a lack of training in grief and loss in educational programs. In 1997 the Institute of Medicine released a report (*Approaching Death: Improving Care at the End of Life*) that documented deficiencies in end-of-life care training including legal, organizational, and economic barriers; a public uncomfortable with discussions about death; and education and training for health care professionals that do not teach knowledge, skills, and attitudes needed to care for dying people (Field & Cassel, 1997).

If you have chosen a profession in which you will be helping people—through teaching, human service administration, human resource management, coaching, rehabilitation therapy, medicine, social work, or even through law or corrections—you need to be prepared to encounter loss and the grief reactions loss engenders.

This book is written for a broad professional audience because loss is encountered everywhere—in hospitals, hospices and skilled nursing facilities, schools, businesses, community clinics, prisons, and in every possible professional setting. You may find yourself coaching a child whose parent or grandparent has died, teaching in a school in which a teacher or student has died, serving as a probation officer to an adolescent whose best friend has been killed, providing legal counsel to a family that has sustained the death of their patriarch, or coordinating home care services in a senior center for an elderly woman whose husband has died and whose children have concerns about her ability to live independently in her home of fifty years.

These represent only a few of the many common types of losses due to death that helping professionals encounter. The examples are quite typical of the kinds of deaths that occur every day in our communities. If you are wondering about what you should gain from this textbook, you should ask yourself the following questions:

- How comfortable and confident am I in my own ability to deal with grief and loss?
- How well do I understand the impact of death on people of different ages, genders, cultures, and spiritual orientations?
- How familiar am I with other life events and losses that can cause grief reactions?

- Am I confident that I can identify when an individual or family is expressing normal grief or when their grief may be complicated?
- How prepared am I to respond effectively to those around me who are grieving?
- Do I know how to acknowledge grief and make a referral to an appropriate resource when necessary?

In addition to preparing you to address grief in reaction to death that you will inevitably encounter in your practice, this text is intended to prepare you to identify and assist individuals and families who may be coping with grief due to causes other than death. Loss and grief are experienced in reaction to divorce, foster care placement, children leaving home for independent living, unemployment, and changes in health status. These types of losses are termed "symbolic losses" and often trigger grief reactions that are similar to those that occur in reaction to death. It is important to be aware of all of the losses that may cause grief reactions in order to respond effectively to those who may need your help.

Symbolic Loss

One student in a loss and grief course shares her experiences with symbolic loss:

> The three most difficult situations that I have had to deal with in my life were divorce, selling my home, and losing my dog. My reaction to my divorce was a terrible feeling of loss. I lost my husband, my role as a wife, my identity, and my last name! I felt like it was a death more than a divorce. It was the worst pain that I have ever encountered in my life! I had to grieve for all of the dreams that will never be met. I had numerous symptoms as a result: weight loss, disturbance in sleep, crying, lack of strength, physical exhaustion, feelings of emptiness and heaviness, indications of anxiety, and lastly, lack of energy (Kroeber, 2004).

Once you have become attuned to loss and grief, you will be better able to recognize and acknowledge when someone is grieving and needs support. It will be important for you to be aware of, and prepared for, grief reactions that you will observe in situations other than death. There are many types of losses that are not due to death, but rather represent the loss of relationships, intact systems, and even dreams for the future.

> Examples of a symbolic (psychological) loss include getting a divorce or losing status because of a job demotion. Usually a symbolic loss is not identified as a loss per se, so we may not realize we need to take the time to grieve and deal with our feelings about it. Nevertheless, it will initiate a process of grief just as a physical loss will (Rando, 1984, p.16).

As this quotation indicates, the same kind of grief reactions that are seen in situations involving death—including the expression of denial, anger, sadness, guilt or shame, as well as eventual acceptance—are also common in symbolic losses. There is a major difference, however, between loss due to death and symbolic losses. Often symbolic losses go unacknowledged by others and therefore the grieving individual does not receive the same kind or amount of support that those grieving a death may receive.

Children placed in foster care, biological and foster parents from whose homes children are removed, families experiencing a difficult divorce, parents whose children have been diagnosed with a disabling medical or mental condition, and even adults whose children are leaving home, or whose parents must be moved from the family home to a nursing home, can be expected to express a variety of grief reactions. They, as well as many others who experience symbolic loss, will need your understanding and will benefit from your ability to listen and provide skilled assistance.

For some readers of this text, acquiring the knowledge and skills included here will enable you to assess what type of grief reaction those you are working with are experiencing and will help prepare you to provide appropriate counseling or therapy based on your assessment. Even if you are not the primary professional directly responsible for providing counseling or psychosocial services, understanding grief and loss will enable you to work collaboratively with, or refer to, a mental health or social services professional specially trained in this area. Whether we are directly providing counseling or not, it is essential for all of us who work with people to be aware of and prepared for responses of individuals, families, and communities who are grieving so that we can work with them effectively.

Loss and Grief in Different Contexts

After many years of teaching social work and providing consultation about grief to a wide variety of programs and agencies, I have come to appreciate how much loss impacts work in every practice setting where professionals are helping others. As a hospital social worker and hospice program director I frequently collaborated with people from other disciplines, so I knew that school guidance counselors, employee assistance program managers, pastoral counselors, and community health providers are almost always closely involved in helping people who grieve when someone dies. But as I began teaching classes on loss to personnel in schools, child welfare agencies, and correctional programs, I realized how important it is for professionals in every discipline to be well prepared to deal with loss and grief—their own as well as others'. Rehabilitation therapists, teachers, child life specialists, and many others encounter loss and grief every day. Unfortunately, many professional training programs do not adequately address issues of grief and loss in their programs. Without sensitization to, and training in, grief and loss, even seasoned mental health professionals may have difficulty identifying and responding effectively to grief-related problems that clients present.

A seasoned crisis counselor pointed out how grief training had helped her become better prepared for her role:

I believe that I have a good idea of my limitations. . . . I know that even with my absolute best efforts, I cannot "cure" someone of his or her grief or the emotional pain. What I can do, however, is offer my help, guidance, advocacy, and care during an incredibly difficult time and help them begin to find their own way out of the pain. If I can make the journey a bit easier, though, that would be success. Three most difficult aspects: First, letting go of (and allowing myself to grieve for) people who have come to be a part of my life. Second, dealing with a certain amount of helplessness. Third, keeping myself in the land of the living when I'm not working—avoiding the tendency to dwell on death. How will I cope? I couldn't possibly do it alone. I will definitely use any support that is available to me—from coworkers or employers, friends, family, etc. I'll have to acknowledge and accept my frustration and stress and grief when they arise. And I'll have to give myself permission to do things I enjoy even when I'm in the midst of death or others' pain (Townsend, 2002).

Grief and loss issues can also sometimes be obscured or neglected in the treatment of clients who present other primary problems when seeking treatment. Professionals who are not attuned to grief issues may miss the opportunity to identify and assist with loss and grief associated with these problems.

Haven and Pearlman (2003), trauma therapists, write about the mourning of a client, a 37-year-old professional woman who had experienced childhood abuse:

The therapy session had focused on Jane's deepening connection with sadness and loss related to her experience as the mother of an adolescent who underwent a forced abortion of a pregnancy resulting from incest. The mourning process had been a frequent focal point over the past year and, although extremely painful, had begun to help Jane experience herself as less toxic and to connect with her strength as a nurturing mother of her teenage daughter. Often during the processing of the abortion, Jane would state with tears, "my heart hurts." The therapist understood and responded to this statement as an expression of loss, a sense of heartbreak (p. 217).

Often in our class discussions, when we begin to discuss the topic of grief, students are immediately able to identify clients they have been working with who have experienced loss and who have been dealing with unacknowledged grief. In response to an exercise similar to the one included at the end of this chapter, one student who works with children in protective custody wrote:

I believe that my own experience of the symbolic loss of a parent puts me in a position to empathize with the children whom I work with, as many of them have lost their parents symbolically to substance use. This assignment gave me a new way of thinking about loss and that these children I work with need to grieve the loss of their parent even if the parent hasn't passed away. They also have to grieve for the loss of many symbolic things when they come into foster care: the ideal of living in a home with their family, their neighborhood, their school relationships, and often their extended family ties (Furmanek, 2004).

A student working with families who had fled rural and arid Somalia and were resettled in an urban center in New England, spoke of the parents she was meeting who were grieving the loss of their homeland, their extended families, and their whole way of life, including a family structure, partly influenced by Muslim beliefs, in which men had primary authority in decision-making as well as income earning. Many authors who have written about vulnerable populations with refugee status have described the difficulties adults from other cultures may have in adapting to American culture. A major challenge for many refugees is the different roles that women carry in the United States, where women frequently participate equally in earning income and decision-making for the family. The differences often require that families give up the role expectations they brought with them. And this kind of change represents a loss, one that refugees must deal with along with the many other losses associated with flight from one's country of origin.

Adult refugees may also grieve the loss of their cultural norms when their children and adolescents adopt the mores of urban American youth (Drachman and Ryan, 2001). Yet, these losses and the grief related to them are not often given expression or acknowledged by families or the professionals who interact with them. Sometimes this is because language barriers create difficulties in communicating about loss, and sometimes it is because the professionals are unaware of the norms and expectations in a country of origin and are therefore unaware of the loss associated with role changes.

Another type of symbolic loss that may go unacknowledged is that experienced by parents when their children leave home as late adolescents or young adults. Kennedy describes the grief reactions of both parents and children in this phase of life:

> The transition to college is a time of excitement, confusion, and anxiety for our kids. It is also the end of a chapter of parenting; the tension can severely strain the parent-child relationship. Many parents experience deep grief as they prepare to let go of their sons and daughters. When an adolescent leaves for college we let go of the child we gave birth to, protected, and nurtured for eighteen years. We will see our child again but we know deep down that the relationship has changed forever. This is a major life passage, one that is not acknowledged in this culture as it should be. Most parents are not prepared to consciously let go of their children. However, we can learn how to nurture a healthy new relationship if we support our kids in their separation, tend to our own grieving, and keep channels of communication open (Kennedy, 2004).

Students and colleagues in allied health, human services, education, law, and social work programs have also provided countless examples of the types of losses that are encountered in the diverse settings in which they carry out their work. My family members have also provided many examples. My father is a retired firefighter who provided emergency care to people coping with many losses over his long career; he saw families who lost their homes and possessions, business owners who lost their means of support, and in the most tragic cases, firefighters and other families who lost loved ones to fire. My sister, an elementary school teacher, has described the sense of loss she experiences when she says goodbye to her students leaving for middle school and launching into adolescence. Another sister is a pediatric physical therapist and we have talked about the many children she has helped to gain mobility after the loss of a limb or the disabling effects of a condition such as cerebral palsy. The children and their parents have often had to deal with multiple or chronic loss—both symbolic and actual. Gitterman (2001) reviews the literature regarding the grief reactions of parents with children diagnosed with disabilities. She writes:

> Unlike parental grieving at the birth of a child with a visible handicap, such as a physical deformity, the process of mourning for a child with a marginal and less observable handicap is prolonged (Killner and Crane, 1979). The parents' reactions are staggered and not clear-cut, as they may move from panic to anger to grief, in any given situation or period of time. How parents react has implications for professional intervention (p.265).

While the role of a physical therapist, like that of the occupational, speech, or respiratory therapist, is primarily to enhance the physical abilities of the individual with a disabling condition, recognizing anger or sadness as part of the grief reaction enables one to be a skilled listener and provider of emotional support. Recognizing these emotions in reaction to their illness is an essential aspect of establishing a therapeutic relationship that will provide effective rehabilitation.

My sister Shirley is a registered dietician who works in a dialysis center. She deals with grief daily. When clients are referred for dialysis, they are coping with the loss or impairment of their kidney functioning. Often they express the same range of emotions in reaction to their illness, and the accompanying losses, that people coping with death express, including denial, anger, sadness, and fear. In addition to the loss of independence that dialysis imposes, many of the people Shirley works with face the loss of their jobs and income (the time and travel required for treatment make many jobs untenable), the loss of their bodily integrity or sense of well-being, and in many instances the loss of cherished leisure or recreational activities and social relationships.

Shirley recently talked about the grief of a 44-year-old man with whom she has been working for several months. Each month she reviews his lab results and counsels him on how he can best manage his diabetes and lab outcomes. He had been employed as a salesman for a manufacturing firm that required regular travel but was unable to continue in this job when dialysis began, as the treatments require three to four hours of travel every other day. Initially his kidneys were partially functioning and he was coping well with the loss of his job and the need to manage his diet and insulin very carefully. However, as the months have passed, his kidneys have ceased to function and he has become increasingly despondent. As is often the case in dialysis, it has become more problematic for him to manage his insulin and his lab results have become more problematic. The more stressed and despondent he has become, the more trouble he has had controlling his eating.

Although the man is receiving counseling and antidepressant medication, Shirley, the clinic dietician, is the primary bearer of news about his lab results and it is inevitable that his feelings of frustration, anger, and sadness come up in their discussions. "He is grieving so many losses," she says. "It's a challenge for me to figure out how to help him focus on achieving good lab results when he's lost his job, his freedom, and his faith. I really understand that he is angry and he needs to express it" (Suter, 2004).

Another professional arena where loss and grief are commonly encountered is the human resource management field. Employees generally call their human resources department with practical questions related to benefits, but they may also express feelings related to grief when seeking information about divorce, substance use, ill family members, or elder care.

Case Example

Ms. O'Connor could be seeking help from the human resources staff of any organization. She is a 57-year-old single woman who has been the caregiver for many years for her 82-year-old father who has Alzheimer's Disease. She has been employed for 25 years by a large insurance agency and has contacted the human resources office there to inquire about her employee benefits, since she is now faced with planning for her father's care during the end stage of his illness. Diagnosed five years before, her father was able to attend a day treatment program while she worked, but in the past six months his symptoms have rapidly accelerated and he now requires full-time care. Ms. O'Connor has come into the human resources office with many questions, including what options she has for family medical leave. She becomes visibly upset as she begins to discuss her father's difficulties and why she needs time from work to care for him, tearfully stating she is not sure how much longer her father can go on. Ms. O'Connor, like most employees faced with this kind of family crisis, is primarily seeking practical help and information from the human resources office. Yet clearly loss and grief are manifested during her conversation with the human resource staff. It is highly likely that months later she will express as much appreciation for the understanding and supportive responses of the staff as for the information she received.

Insurance case managers, legal aid providers, and many other professionals will encounter similar situations in their work. Understanding the meaning of these types of symbolic losses and providing effective responses to individuals who are grieving them is a skill set that every professional needs. In many settings, such as skilled nursing facilities, child care centers, and after-school programs, children and adolescents, as well as adults, often express grief in reaction to symbolic losses. An intern in a skilled nursing facility wrote about one type of loss experienced by family members of those afflicted with Alzheimer's:

I observe the child visitor huddling behind the parent, grabbing onto a sleeve, poking his fingers in his mouth, as he peers at the patients with fear. The child brightens as he spies his grandfather and darts out to him. The startled grandfather grabs at the child's arm and pushes him away. The child begins to cry. . . The child is now visiting their grandparent in a hospital. Grandpa may or may not recognize the child, who has a sense of attachment to the familiar family figure who no longer interacts in the same way. I consider the reactions of children unprepared for the reality of Alzheimer's Disease to be strongly equated to the mourning process associated with death. In an attempt to avoid such scenarios, I attempt to discuss the possible reaction of children with the parents before they arrive at the facility. I do not discourage the presence of children on the unit. I do encourage preparation. I want the family to be safe and secure and to benefit from meaningful interaction with their loved one. I also want the child to have an understanding of the person that Grandpa now is (Laudette, 2003).

A worker in a residential foster care facility discussed a client whose story is similar to that of many children that foster care workers, teachers, probation officers, and other human service workers will encounter. The 14-year-old girl had been placed in a therapeutic group home for adolescents. Her mother died in a car accident when she was a toddler. Her father was incarcerated at the time. With no parents to care for her, she and her sister were moved from family member to family member as well as to foster homes where she was sexually and physically abused. Her frequent expressions of anger and poor behavior resulted in residential placement, outside of the city in which she had spent her childhood and separate from her sister. In a secure environment, and with the support of staff at the group home, she was gradually beginning to talk about the many issues of loss she had been struggling with for twelve years. She had not received grief counseling prior to the residential placement, even though she had suffered the death of her mother and many other subsequent losses including the symbolic loss of her biological family, the loss of her childhood, and the loss of the many potential parents and families she experienced through impermanent and destructive foster care placements.

Unfortunately, many children in foster care are not provided with therapeutic grief interventions and secure attachment opportunities during or after placement. These children often develop complicated grief reactions and are frequently labeled with a mental disorder such as reactive attachment disorder, depression, or oppositional defiant disorder. It is especially important for those of us who work with children in foster care to ensure that their losses are recognized and their grief is addressed appropriately. Enabling them to express their understandable feelings of anger, sadness, and anxiety related to loss, and providing them with outlets for grief and stress relief can provide them with a crucial sense of being understood and cared for, and can contribute to healthy future relationships, motivation, and positive self perceptions.

A child protective worker, after participating in a course in loss and bereavement, wrote:

In the work that I do every day it is often difficult to engage a child and get them invested in their treatment because they are, understandably, so angry that they have been taken away from their parents and, of course, the child believes that it is the caseworker's fault that they have been removed. Stabilization into a foster home is probably the most difficult part of the child's treatment and must precede working on disruptive behaviors and other clinical issues. This can be a lengthy process because, in a way, the child first needs to do the grief work around the transition out of their home and the separation between them and their "family." It appears to me to be very similar to having to deal with a deceased loved one, only that these important people still exist and there is always hope in the child's mind that reunification will occur if treatment goals are reached. Part of treatment for them is like any grief work and involves acknowledging and supporting them in processing the feelings of disbelief, anger, and sadness that they are experiencing (Baron, 2002).

This example addresses the grief from the symbolic loss that foster care placement engenders for children and the witnessing of this grief by child protective workers who are charged with assisting them. The grief that families and workers experience that results from family violence, and sometimes death, is also important to recognize. In one of the few professional articles written on this topic, Dr. Michael Durfee (1997) notes in a Web-based publication for the International Child Abuse Network, "Most survivors of fatal child abuse/neglect receive little intervention following such a death. Some sibling survivors may receive counseling for behavior problems. Few are allowed to express their understanding of death. Very few are followed for the first critical year. Many are ignored, even undetected" (p. 1).

The National Resource Center for Respite and Crisis Care Services is funded by the U.S. Department of Health and Human Services, the Administration for Children and Families, and other organizations. In its fact sheet on grief, several different types of symbolic losses are addressed. "The family of a child considered medically fragile who is in need of respite care may experience a sense of loss over not having a 'healthy' or 'perfect' child. The spouse of a family member with Alzheimer's may grieve the loss of the life they have planned together" (Braza, 2002).

This publication emphasizes that all losses, those from death as well as symbolic losses, need to be grieved. It also underscores that professionals with knowledge of grief and how to assist someone in the process will be better able to work effectively with individuals and families in need. Subsequent chapters in this text are designed to provide you with this set of knowledge and skills. Additional resources on the topics covered in this chapter and subsequent chapters can be found through the Internet Resources listed near the end of this chapter and are linked to the companion Web site for this text at www.ablongman.com.

Although the world is full of suffering, it is full also of the overcoming of it.

—Helen Keller

Exercise: Identifying Loss and Grief _____

This exercise is intended to help you identify the kinds of losses and grief reactions you may encounter in your internship or practice setting. You can complete this as an individual exercise or a classroom exercise in your training program.

- If completed as an individual, use a piece of notebook paper and a pen.
- If completed in the classroom, break into small groups of 3, 4, or 5 students.
- Use large sheets of self-adhesive flip-chart paper or large newsprint sheets that can be displayed on the wall with masking tape (one for each group of students) and wide-tipped felt markers so the writing will be visible to all. When steps 1 through 3 have been completed, post the sheets around the room and complete step 4 as a class.

1. Write on the top of the sheet the types of settings you and your group members are currently working in or hope to work in. Divide the rest of the sheet into two columns.
2. In the first column, write down the types of losses, both actual and symbolic, that clients you are working with are likely to experience. (For example, if the setting is a school, actual losses might be the death of a faculty member and symbolic losses might include children whose parents are divorcing.)
3. In the second column, write the emotions someone experiencing each loss is likely to experience.
4. Discuss your thoughts about how you might observe these losses and the feelings related to them in each work setting. (For example, a school counselor leading a group for children whose parents are divorcing might observe academic performance problems with some of the children.)

Self-Test

1. Which of the following is NOT considered a symbolic loss?
   a. A death in the family
   b. Separation of the family due to divorce
   c. Separation from family due to foster care placement
   d. Diagnosis of a disabling medical condition such as Alzheimer's Disease

2. True or False: Symbolic losses often generate the same types of grief reactions as loss due to death.

3. Children who are placed in foster care due to abuse often experience complicated grief in reaction to:
   a. The death of a parent
   b. The symbolic loss of their biologic family
   c. Frequent changes in caseworkers
   d. Chronic illness such as ADHD

Answers: 1) a   2) True   3) b

Internet Resources

Because of the constantly changing content of the Web, it is impossible to ensure that links listed in a printed text will be up to date. Current links for this chapter and subsequent chapters can be found on the companion Web site for this text which can be accessed at www.ablongman.com.

Some of these include:

The National Resource Center for Respite and Crisis Care Services provides many useful information sheets. ARCH encourages readers to copy and make use of them, but to credit ARCH when doing so. (http://www.archrespite.org/ARCHfact.htm)

References

Baron, K. (2002). *Loss and bereavement journal*. Springfield, MA: Springfield College School of Social Work.

Braza, K. (2002). Families and the grief process. *ARCH National Resource Center for Crisis Nurseries and Respite Care Services, Factsheet Number 21*. Retrieved January 10, 2002 from http://www.archrespite.org/archfs21.htm.

Drachman, D., & Ryan, A. S. (2001). Immigrants and refugees. In A. Gitterman (Ed.) *Handbook of social work practice with vulnerable and resilient populations* (pp. 651–686). New York: Columbia University Press.

Durfee, M. (1997). Facing the issues: Grief and mourning. International Child Abuse Network. Retrieved January, 25, 2004 from http://66.127.183.74/articles/grmourn.html.

Field, M. J., & Cassel, C. K. (1997). *Approaching death: Improving care at the end of life*. Washington, DC: National Academies Press.

Furmanek, R. (2004). *Loss and bereavement journal*. Springfield, MA: Springfield College School of Social Work.

Gitterman. (2001). Learning disabilities. In A. Gitterman (Ed.) *Handbook of social work practice with vulnerable and resilient populations* (pp. 249–274). New York: Columbia University Press.

Haven, T. J., & Pearlman, L. A. (2003). Minding the body: The intersection of dissociation and physical health in relational trauma psychotherapy. In K.A. Kendall-Tackett (Ed.) *Health consequences of abuse in the family: A clinical guide for evidence-based practice* (pp. 215–232). Washington, DC: American Psychological Association.

Kennedy, A. (2004). Empty nest, full heart. Workshop presented July 14, 2001 at UCSC Extension. Retrieved January 10, 2004 from http://www.alexandrakennedy.com.

Killner, S. K., & Crane, R. (1979). A parental dilemma: The child with a marginal handicap. *Social Casework 60*(1), 30–35.

Kroeber, N. (2004). *Loss and bereavement journal*. Springfield, MA: Springfield College School of Social Work.

Laudette, S. (2003). *Loss and bereavement journal*. Springfield, MA: Springfield College School of Social Work.

Rando, T. (1984). *Grief, dying and death: Clinical interventions for caregivers*. Champaign, IL: Research Press Company.

Suter, S. (2004). Personal communication in Cincinnati, Ohio, November 15, 2003.

Townsend, M. (2002). *Loss and bereavement journal*. Springfield, MA: Springfield College School of Social Work.

2

Self-Preparation and Training for Professionals Encountering Loss and Grief

Topics

Reviewing Our Own Experiences and Attitudes Related to Grief

Assessing and Enhancing Readiness to Address Grief in Our Work

Supervision, Consultation, and Collaboration with Other Professionals

> *Everything that happens to you is your teacher. The secret is to sit at the feet of your own life and be taught by it.*
>
> —Polly B. Berends

Reviewing Our Own Experiences and Attitudes Related to Grief

Can you remember the very first death of someone close to you or the first significant symbolic loss in your life? Some people, when asked this question, can retrieve a memory quite quickly. Some may recall the death of a grandparent or even a pet. Others recall learning that their parents were divorcing. Even if one's own personal losses have been limited, many people who were children when President John F. Kennedy was assassinated or when the space shuttle Challenger exploded can recall vividly these deaths as well as the reactions of those around them. More recently, almost everyone in the United States can recall their reactions to the deaths of the more than 3,000 victims of the World Trade Towers and Pentagon terrorist attacks on

September 11, 2001. Death and loss in our contemporary, media-saturated culture is unavoidable. Yet, it is only recently that we have begun to include training in grief in many educational programs and to attend to the emotional impact that loss and grief have on us as professionals.

It is important to review our own experiences with loss in order to understand and respond effectively to the grief of others. However, it is also essential to ensure that we are adequately aware of, and attending to, our own grief. Almost every text-book or course about grief begins with an exploration of one's own losses. As an instructor, I assign the exercise included at the end of this chapter to students in my Loss and Grief courses. While they find it a very challenging assignment, they also unanimously report that it is useful in preparing them to help others. Students often make comments such as:

> "This exercise has helped me look at my own losses as well as those of my clients and understand them on a whole new level."
> "I am clearer as to why I have avoided people who are dealing with death and grief and I feel prepared to deal with them in a different way now."
> "Having to recollect some of the details that happened when I experi-enced a loss in my childhood was heart wrenching, but I have been able to place some of that bereavement in its proper place. The exercise has also made me realize that there are some issues I haven't addressed that I need to."

As discussed in Chapter 1, grief is a reaction to many different types of losses, not only loss through death. Even if you have not yet experienced the death of a sig-nificant person in your life, you have most likely experienced the loss of a relation-ship or other symbolic loss that will impact your reactions to the losses of others. Not surprisingly, older and younger students alike report that through self-exploration, they identify issues related to loss in their own personal and professional lives that have had a major impact. The exercise has helped many to complete their own griev-ing process and better equip them to cope with grief and loss in their families and their workplaces.

One student offered her thoughts about this process in a class discussion. She said she had only been to two funerals in her life. Holding a wake and then a funeral was the way that her ethnic group practiced a funeral ritual. During the class, she real-ized she had always been afraid of death so she avoided funerals as much as she could. Reflecting on what she had observed in her two experiences attending them, however, she recognized that viewing the body and accepting the condolences of others seemed to be helpful to the mourners. She said that taking the class had helped her sort out a lot of unresolved and unanswered issues about death and loss. She stated her intention to continue to deal with and sort out her own feelings, believing that it would better prepare her to help others in the internship she had signed up for in a hospital.

Many students have expressed similar feelings and fears about studying grief and loss, but they have subsequently realized the personal and professional benefits of tackling this difficult subject. Others have decided to study grief and loss or to work specifically in this area because they have found meaning through loss in their own lives and now want to help others.

A student who had worked through many of her own personal losses in an undergraduate course in death and dying chose to work in a hospice program assisting patients and families. She also entered a social work master's degree program to advance her knowledge and skills. In response to the exercise she wrote:

> Although going through the grief process has its ups and downs, the more aware you are of what to expect, the easier you are on yourself. I have not yet had a negative experience coping with loss. I am well aware that I am only 25, and that I will experience a lot more losses; some may be negative while others are positive. While working with dying patients and the bereaved, I have learned that everyone is unique and responds to loss differently and on an individual basis. I go in on every case with a clean sheet—understanding that each family system and the dynamics between people and relationships vary from each person. Also, each person is unique in their thoughts on death and dying. The more a professional learns about the people they are working with, the easier it is to help and assist them through the process. This fits with my issues related to death and loss because I know that learning about death and dying will never end for me, and that people's experiences and life lessons help in teaching me something new about death and dying (Hdlacki, 2004).

Gerry, Gail, David, Lorenzo, Helen, Bill . . . these are the names of only a handful of the hundreds of people who have touched my own life through my work as an oncology social worker. Theirs are the faces that I see as clearly today as I did five or ten or twenty years ago when I first met each of them. Lorenzo was a young college student who came to the large Boston cancer center where I had recently begun to work at the age of 24, and he was the first person to look me in the eye and tell me he was afraid to die. He was 22-years-old and had just learned that the acute lymphocytic leukemia that had initially struck during his freshman year in college had reoccurred. I wasn't much older than he was at the time and still remember how acutely inadequate I felt in trying to respond to his fear.

Forty year-old Bill, his wife, and five children shared with me their hopes for one more Christmas together in one of our many family meetings. Bill had melanoma that had traveled to his brain and he was committed to preparing his wife and children for the possibility of his death. His 10-year-old daughter, Chrissy, said to me, "I want my father to be alive for Christmas and also for my birthday." Bill lived for both but died shortly after, leaving his wife Yvonne, Chrissy, and her four brothers and sisters without a husband and father. While our interdisciplinary team couldn't help Bill live longer, we did succeed in helping to make the time he spent together with his family very meaningful.

Gerry was a high school guidance counselor. Helen was a mother of eight. Gail, who I first met in the twentieth year of my oncology career, was a mother just my age, with two daughters the same ages as my two daughters, when she died after a hard fought battle with breast cancer. I had the privilege of meeting each of them at a time when impending loss made time and relationships seem more precious.

The close contact with loss has affected both my work and my personal life in different ways at different times. At a St. Patrick's Day parade, crouched on a curb with my two young daughters, waving our flags and shamrocks at the passing dignitaries and laughing at the Melha Shriners in their tiny cars skittering wildly across the road, the combined reminders of hospitals and limousines would take my mind back to the funeral I attended for Gerry, an exceptionally popular high school guidance counselor. It seemed like hundreds of us were lined up in the procession behind a long line of limousines carrying dozens of grief stricken family members to the funeral. At the church, which could not hold all of the mourners, many of us stood on the steps outside, straining to hear his students speaking in his honor about the unfairness of losing their mentor. Then, my small daughter tugged on my arm and brought my thoughts back to the parade.

In a social group of young mothers, each of us pushing our toddlers on swings and sharing views on local pediatricians, the image of a stoic 17-year-old boy from timber country in rural Maine, uprooted by leukemia and transplanted to Boston, would suddenly be with me. I would remember him valiantly plodding the hallways of the transplant center pushing his IV pole on wheels in his hospital gown. His once muscular legs moved like shortened stilts—slowly and laboriously, his mother by his side. I would flash back to the look of bewilderment on his face when the oncology fellow who'd aggressively and optimistically offered one potential solution after another that we all clung to, finally admitted, "we can try to keep you comfortable . . ." In my memory I could almost feel my hand supporting his mother as her legs folded under her at the news. Then I would refocus and be back with the group in my backyard, pushing my own baby in her swing.

Inevitably, certain losses would remind me of deaths in my own family. The memory of our ten-month-old niece's death from SIDS and my sister-in-law's wrenching grief could be activated by seeing a mother's reaction to her child's death, and every elderly man could evoke the hollow feeling of emptiness I felt at the death of my grandfather, who had been a mentor to me.

At times, over the years, when the impact of these losses has felt overwhelming, I have asked myself whether I could continue to become so close to people—especially other families—facing death. How many more painful memories could I accumulate? At times I have cried in my car all the way home from the hospital or a client's home, the tears triggered by a song on the radio or a simple public service announcement. When this has happened, I have thought about changing jobs—giving up the intense emotional challenges of witnessing death and weathering grief. At other times I, like many professionals in the field, would give less than all of myself out of fear that I wouldn't be able to bear any more anguish. I read articles on burnout and compassion fatigue and questioned the wisdom of continuing, thinking maybe it was time for a break or maybe it was time to give up my career as a social worker. Fortunately, I have had the benefit of excellent consultation from my supervisors and colleagues, attended many professional development programs, and participated in peer support sessions where I could talk about these feelings and thoughts. I have also derived a great deal of inspiration from the grieving people I have come to know in my work.

One example of such inspiration came from a breast cancer survivor who invited me to a reading of her poetry. She is gifted with the ability to express herself through poetry and had written her way through multiple surgeries and chemotherapy treatments, the loss of her hair and all of the indignities and terrors one must endure when cancer wreaks its havoc. As a celebration marking her fifth year of survival she arranged a beautiful ceremony, inviting family, old friends, and new acquaintances made during her treatment. She treated us all to delicious food and then read poems aloud from her book, *Feeling Light in the Dark* (Walker, 1997).

Here is one of her poems:

Post-op Surgery Six

I raise my arm above my head,
Pulling from the heart which has been
Above it all.
Now it stops, as final as death.

There is no chance, or thought
To be Superwoman
No temptation to push a little harder,
Or defy the odds.

I have never known
The fragility of my own cells.
The starkness of reality, without denial,
Is terrifying.

It was encouraging to be at this celebration of life with this woman, and others, who had endured so much. As we gathered in a circle following her reading, she invited everyone to think of an affirmation in response to whatever emotions the reading and the celebration had elicited in us. We held hands and as I looked around the circle at all of the people who felt connected to this woman through cancer, including myself, I was reminded of a quote I heard at a grief counseling training workshop. It sustained me then and has continued to sustain me in the past eight years since this ceremony:

Nobody has ever measured, even poets, how much a heart can hold.

—Zelda Fitzgerald

It is a simple affirmation but I repeat it whenever I need inspiration to get through difficult times. Jackie Walker, the poet, is now the co-founder and director of an organization in our community, Cancer Connection, that provides support to other survivors. I have the privilege of serving on the organization's professional advisory board. Jackie and I both create meaning from our losses through helping others. I have come to think of the human heart not as a container for emotions, with limits and boundaries and a defined area that can be overfilled. Instead, I think of our hearts as the part of each of us that connects us to others, giving and receiving the life force that sustains us in human relationships. I believe that in order to work effectively with others who are sustaining losses we must do what Marion Stonberg (1980), a leader in the field of oncology social work, advises us to do—both listen *to* our hearts and listen *with* our hearts.

Our own losses can revisit and often surprise us, triggered by a familiar smell, expression, or experience. We need to acknowledge the feelings related to these losses and yet allow ourselves to be free enough to experience new feelings for new people and relationships. If we can learn to do this, we can do the important work of helping others do the same.

Assessing and Enhancing Readiness to Address Grief in Our Work

How do we know if we are ready to help others with their grief?

> *What is of greatest importance in a person's life is not just the nature and extent of his or her experiences but what has been learned from them.*
>
> —Norman Cousins

Our own thoughts, feelings, and beliefs inevitably impact the way we approach those who are experiencing grief. Therefore, self-assessment and self-awareness is important for every professional who interacts with others experiencing loss. This includes physical, speech, respiratory, and occupational therapists working with those who have experienced the loss of bodily integrity that comes from stroke, auto accidents, or war injury. It also includes teachers, probation officers, and residential group home workers who encounter children who have sustained the loss of family through death, foster care placement, divorce, or even the fleeing of one's country of origin to escape political oppression.

What memories or experiences in our own lives are likely to be activated when we hear of these losses? What physical and emotional reactions in our bodies, our minds, or our hearts give us clues that we are reacting to our own losses as well as theirs? As you proceed through the chapters that follow and learn more about the somatic (physical), psychological, social, and spiritual reactions to loss that are common in those who are grieving, think about your own losses and how you have dealt with them in body, mind, and spirit. Did you feel intense fatigue? If so, you can appreciate the physical and emotional exhaustion of your own clients or students who are grieving. If you experienced road rage or direct feelings of anger after a loss, you may also understand the angry acting-out behavior that some grieving children, adolescents, and even adults exhibit. If you avoided or denied feelings, your acknowledgement of the denial may help you to recognize when others may be in denial or having difficulty expressing their most painful feelings.

The more aware we are of our own feelings and reactions, the more we will be able to identify when a client's situation is making us feel uncomfortable and what to do about it. On the positive side, self-awareness can also increase our capacity to understand and empathize with the unique responses of others to loss. Bill Moyers helped many of us in America think about issues of dying and loss in his PBS series *On Our Own Terms.* The Web site for the program offers a wealth of information and resources to both professionals and the public. You may wish to use the link to this site (provided in the Internet Resources section of this chapter and on the companion Web site for the text) to complete an interactive self-assessment of your own. In addition, a self-assessment exercise is included at the end of this chapter to get you started. As with other exercises and experiential learning tools in this text, you may want to complete the self-assessment exercise now, before moving on to the next topic for this chapter. Take the time you need to reflect on your own experiences. Give yourself some space and privacy as well. If the feelings that arise are difficult for you, or you find it really challenging, it may be useful to talk with someone who can listen empathically and provide support to you. You may be able to get support from a close and trusted friend or partner, but it may also be useful to talk with a professional grief counselor.

Although it may be difficult to think back to early losses and recall the feelings associated with them, it is essential to deal with your own feelings of grief before you can be effective in helping others. Feelings associated with death are not the only grief reactions you need to be aware of. If there is a history of substance dependence or addiction, conflicted divorce, emotional cut-offs with family or friends, child custody issues, job loss, or other unresolved symbolic losses in your past, the emotions associated with these can be activated when working closely with others and are best dealt with prior to encountering loss in the lives of those you hope to help.

Working with individuals and families facing loss inevitably brings up emotions and memories for every professional.

Most people who choose to work with others have chosen their work because they genuinely want to help others. Many establish strong connections with the people they work with and need to grieve when facing the loss of these relationships. This can be difficult because many patients and families facing slowly progressive or chronic diseases, or those with injuries that are not immediately life threatening, are not able to directly acknowledge their reactions to loss. Similarly, people experiencing significant symbolic losses, such as the diagnosis of a child with a serious medical condition or disability, may not be aware that they are experiencing grief and may not acknowledge their feelings directly. They may react initially with denial or anger, common reactions which will be discussed more fully in the next several chapters. This can make our work with them more challenging. Understanding their reactions, as well as our own, makes it possible for us to reach out and help, despite the challenges. One seasoned substance abuse counselor discusses how grief and loss enter into his work and professional practice:

> Reading about grief has forced me to reflect on the deaths of clients that I have built therapeutic relationships with during the course of my work as a substance abuse counselor. Although I maintain a professional therapeutic relationship with clients, its is still a relationship, nonetheless. The reason that these relationships become so intense is because I have been working for the same company for over ten years, and have worked in all of our available modalities of treatment: outpatient for two years, inpatient treatment for one year, half-way house manager/counselor for three years, and detox/evaluation for four years. During this time I have worked with a lot of clients, but most of the clients are repeaters, coming through detox or treatment, in many cases, multiple times. Therefore there are many clients that I have known for my entire ten-year experience. The reason this is so pertinent to this discussion is that sometimes they die. At one point over the years, the death of clients was so regular that our long-term facility ceased taking clients who were high-risk. One client, for example, either walked, fell, or was pushed in front of a train. The circumstances of his demise are still unknown. In our detox facility, clients are in and out multiple times until one day they just don't come back. Eventually, someone will recognize the name in the newspaper obituaries or hear about the death in an Alcoholics Anonymous meeting. A lot of times the news of the fatality is passed on to us by a returning client.
>
> Worden (2002) states that a counselor can avoid burnout by practicing 'active grieving.' I practice active grieving often. The death of a client affects me in multiple ways. First, I wonder if there is more I could have done that would have made a difference; second, I become angry, thinking how senseless the death was and how it could have been avoided if the client would have gone through treatment on their previous detox; third, I go through what Worden describes as 'existential anxiety,' or awareness of my own mortality. Fortunately, I have found ways to process my thoughts and emotions related to the loss (Ward, 2003).

This professional helper has clearly confronted and dealt with the many types of losses encountered in his work. An issue for many grief specialists, however, is the lack of attention to, and support for, those who are grieving in work places—especially in institutions and organizations that provide services to individuals and families who are grieving. Many times these organizations *fail to provide supports to their own staff for processing grief.*

Paul Brenner (1999) attributes this to the medical model that is practiced within many organizations, even health care agencies, in which death is viewed as the enemy and therefore the needs of grieving staff are acknowledged only through a very brief bereavement leave, with little or no formal support for processing grief. He suggests that institutions and agencies must create a new culture that trains and supports staff in grief and grief care.

Therese Rando (1984) also points to the organizational constraints that make it difficult for professional helpers who work with those who are dying or grieving.

> There is a lack of behavioral operationalization that is always needed in ambiguous circumstances. In addition, when there is a lack of understanding of the necessary mourning and grieving that occur when patients die, caregivers may feel that they have somehow failed by experiencing such reactions, when in fact these are completely normal and expected (p. 437).

We would expect that training and support for professional caregivers' grief would be provided in hospitals, medical settings, and other organizations that frequently deal with loss. Yet often it is not. Training and support may be even less available in other organizations in which death or loss is not as frequent an occurrence, or where the losses are more symbolic, like substance abuse treatment settings. The child welfare field is another practice arena in which both actual and symbolic losses are prevalent. Child protective workers are expected to support children who are experiencing the loss of a biological parent, sometimes through foster care placement, yet these workers are rarely provided training or adequate time to assist children or families with grief reactions.

One child protective worker wrote about the grief she had become aware of in foster children and their biological parents, while taking a graduate course on grief and loss. She notes:

> Children grieve the loss of many symbolic things when they come into foster care, including the ideal of living in a home with your family, their neighborhood, their school relationships, as well as many times extended family ties. The same is true for parents who lose a child due to child protection issues. These individuals are blamed for the removal and do not obtain the same type of support as someone who lost their child to a tragic accident. The fact is that once a child is removed by social services it is many times a permanent loss, just as if a child had passed away. I believe these factors greatly influence a person's ability to mourn, as they are many times not going to receive support, they may have ambivalent feelings about the person who is gone or is dying due to these stigmas, and they are more prone to isolate out of embarrassment or fear of what others will think (Furmanek, 2004).

Often those who receive the least support for their grief are helping professionals themselves, whose employers, or even coworkers, do not acknowledge their grief. Guidelines and methods for assessing and assisting with grief reactions are included in subsequent chapters. These are applicable both to helping professionals and to clients. Increasing awareness and acknowledgment of our feelings related to grief is the first step to providing care to others. The next step is equipping ourselves with the knowledge and skills that will make our work with others who are grieving more effective. Hopefully, after reading this book, you will have ideas about how this can be done, both for yourself and for those in your employment or practice setting.

Establishing competence in providing care to those who are grieving.

Supportive Care of the Dying (SCD) is an advocacy organization involved in a national initiative to improve care and services to those who are dealing with dying and death in America. This organization, along with others, has begun to establish standards and competencies for end of life care for professionals and organizations. Grief care is included in the concept of end of life care, since those who are anticipating the end of life, as well as those who have experienced a death, experience grief.

'Tools for Change' is a set of assessment tools that are available on the organization's Web site. (The link for this site is listed in the Internet Resources section of this chapter and can be found on the companion Web site for this text). Competencies have been established in the physical, spiritual, emotional, relationship, and communication realms of care. These competencies can serve as an important self-check to determine readiness to help in the arena of grief. For example, competence in the emotional aspects of care include the ability to:

- Support clients in their expression of emotional needs
- Actively listen
- Refer to support groups, peer support programs, and professional experts
- Ask open-ended questions such as "how are you doing?"

(www.supportivecareforthedying.org, accessed June 29, 2004.)

Many professional organizations have also established standards or competencies for those who practice in specific disciplines such as nursing, physical therapy, education, and social work. These competencies often inform the criteria for professional credentialing and questions related to them can be found in the licensing exams for many professions. For example, questions designed to measure competence in end of life care, which includes grief, are included in the nursing licensing examinations in many states. Awareness of the competencies and the competency requirements for your profession is therefore extremely important.

While some allied health professions, such as nursing and social work, have established competencies in the arena of end of life care, those outside the health field may not yet specifically address grief and loss. However, as a result of September 11th and other tragedies that have affected whole communities, many organizations now provide resources to enhance the professional development and effectiveness of professionals who work in a wide range of community agencies. For example, the National Education Association has developed a Web page entitled Crisis Tools for Schools that includes descriptions of the roles of school personnel in managing a crisis. Chapter 7 in this text provides specific information about how professionals can facilitate coping in traumatic grief situations and the Web links for that chapter and Chapter 8 provide additional resources for increasing professional capacity and competence.

It is also always useful to contact the professional organization in your discipline to see what competencies have been established and what training resources they offer. The companion Web site for this textbook includes links to resources offered by some professional organizations. Chapters 6 and 8 will provide some basic skills and strategies that you can use as well.

Supervision, Consultation, and Collaboration with Other Professionals

Supervision, consultation, and collaboration are important in all helping professionals' work. However, they can be especially important when we are working with clients who have experienced trauma or loss. Supervision provides an opportunity to assess, in an ongoing way, both the effectiveness of our work and the effect the work has on us. Most of us, during training internships, have the benefit of supervision and consultation with experienced staff in our own disciplines who can answer our questions, provide information and expertise, and address concerns about our work. In the teaching profession many systems include "Master Teachers," seasoned classroom instructors who provide modeling and consultation to those newer to the profession, in addition to the modeling and consultation that occur during teacher training experiences.

In social work, education, and other professions, supervision and consultation can be used to examine the feelings and thoughts that we experience as we interact with others in distress. It is especially important to seek the help of a supervisor when our exposure to the distress of others is prolonged, frequent, or intense. Staff in long-term care and emergency room settings, inner city schools, child protective, and residential treatment settings are among those who work with students and clients who are repeatedly exposed to trauma and loss, and thus may experience **vicarious trauma** or **secondary trauma** with repeated or intense exposure to others' losses.

Vicarious trauma, or secondary trauma, is now recognized as *a common reaction in professionals who work closely with individuals or groups who have directly experienced trauma.* Child protective workers who hear graphic details of child abuse, teachers who read what their students have written about traumatic events, and health care workers who witness the traumatic physical and emotional effects of illness and injury are all likely to experience some degree of secondary trauma and experience grief reactions as a result. Supervisors, peers, and consultants can help us to recognize when our own reactions may be distressed. This is important because we may not always recognize when our avoidance, anger, or tearfulness is a reaction to the distress we have witnessed in our clients or students. Supervision and consultation can also help us to identify strategies to make the best use of our knowledge, skills, and natural helping instincts and to manage our own stress as well as the stress of those we are helping.

One student's internship at a women's prison brought her into close contact with inmates whose lives had been filled with losses—loss due to deaths of family and friends, loss of their children to protective service placements, loss of their free-dom and sense of personal self-efficacy, and even losses of the close relationships some formed in prison. A survey of the inmates at the women's prison unit conducted during the intern's year revealed that almost all of the inmates had also experienced trauma in their lives. Many had experienced multiple traumas including childhood abuse and domestic violence. The intern found that hearing about the inmates' trauma and loss activated strong feelings in her—feelings related to her own life as well as the losses these women had sustained. In her loss and bereavement journal she wrote:

> I learned quickly at the jail. It was such a drastic change from anything else I ever experienced; I would have been lost without the help of my supervisor and fellow workers (Kirkland, 2003).

Rando (1984) writes about the importance of developing an awareness of our own energy levels.

> I am just beginning to learn my emotional limitations. It is critical to avoid comparing my needs to others and recognize my need for a break or a 'time-out'.

In addition to the consultation and support that is provided through supervision, in most settings professionals also work alongside professionals from other disciplines who are a source of consultation and mutual support. Many times work with other dis-ciplines occurs in the context of a formal **multidisciplinary** or **interdisciplinary** team. The term interdisciplinary team is often used now to describe *a team of profes-sionals from different disciplines who have a formal structure for active communica-tion and collaboration in developing a comprehensive plan and carrying it out.* The term multidisciplinary team is generally used in *settings in which there is not a for-mally established structure, such as a team meeting, to facilitate communication and collaboration among team members,* but there is acknowledgement that a variety of professionals and paraprofessionals from different disciplines may be working to help a single client, patient, or student to achieve goals. In this type of setting, emphasis is on the *multiple* disciplines in the system rather than on *interdisciplinary* communica-tion. It is an important distinction because it may be more challenging for the profes-sionals working in a multidisciplinary setting to have direct communication with one another. In the absence of a team meeting or other formal structure for collaboration that is often present in an interdisciplinary team setting, individual team members may have to take more initiative to communicate and collaborate with other specialists.

In many medical settings the interdisciplinary team often includes a physician, nurse, social worker, rehabilitation therapists, pharmacist, chaplain, and other allied health professionals. These team members communicate through a formal charting or documentation system and often collaborate through a formal team meeting or team rounds. In a school setting the multidisciplinary team may include teachers, guidance counselors or school social workers, attendance specialists, and disciplinary staff or administrative personnel. In some school settings interdisciplinary teams function in the arena of special education and formal meetings do occur to create and monitor an Individual Education Plan (IEP), bringing together classroom teachers, special education teachers, and rehabilitation specialists such as physical, occupational, speech, and language therapists, in addition to the guidance personnel. In corrections and child welfare settings the team may not be formally structured or even referred to formally as a team, but lawyers, parole or probation officers, child welfare workers, and psychologists or addictions specialists may all be involved in working with a single client, and therefore frequently communicate or collaborate with one another. Each of these presents opportunities for you to both seek and provide information and support related to the grief you or your clients or students experience.

The benefit of many different professionals working to achieve client goals is that each member of the team contributes expertise to the treatment (or education) plan. If you are a mental health counselor, psychologist, social worker, or guidance counselor on the team, you may be the person who carries out the grief assessment and provides expert information to the team on reactions to loss. Other team members may also look to you for support or information about their own grief reactions. Not all members of the team are expected to work directly to address emotional concerns like those associated with loss.

Each professional helper must be prepared to understand and respond effectively to the various types of distress expressed by those we are trying to help. This is particularly true when a death or significant loss is causing distress, because each of us plays an important role in helping clients or students achieve their goals and everyone is likely to encounter emotional reactions in carrying out our roles and functions. For example, occupational and physical therapists, like teachers, need to be prepared to listen supportively and help problem-solve when emotional distress is evident, and in particular, when it negatively impacts their patients' or students' ability to carry out important tasks such as academic endeavors or activities of daily living.

Similarly, professionals in the legal arena may find that unresolved grief may be making it impossible for their client to move toward necessary change. An elderly client, for example, who is facing multiple losses and experiencing complicated grief, may appear to have memory deficits that bring competency into question. Adolescents experiencing traumatic losses may act out aggressively or withdraw and be unable to effectively perform school or work-related tasks until their grief issues are addressed. Chapters 3 and 4 will review grief reactions that are considered by grief experts to be *normal* and *complicated* responses for individuals at different stages of the life span and from different cultural backgrounds. This information will enable you to respond more effectively to those who have sustained losses. It is important to remember that there are many sources of help for you, your students, clients, and organizations. Acknowledging your own need for additional information or emotional support is essential to professional growth and is an important step in professional development.

Often, when case histories are shared in an interdisciplinary team context, social workers or other mental health professionals can help to identify when grief reactions are in evidence and can recommend specific interventions to address them. Every professional, however, who is attuned to the various manifestations of grief can make an effective intervention through acknowledging loss and the distress they observe in reaction to it. Often this goes a long way toward establishing an effective working relationship in which you are viewed as someone who understands. In addition, being attuned to and acknowledging grief can enable you to help a client or student get expert help when needed. Sharing important information with other disciplines and making referrals when necessary is an important kind of interdisciplinary collaboration that can be carried out in any setting, even in the absence of a formal 'team'.

More information about specific interventions for grief and the roles of various disciplines is included in Chapters 6 and 7. Chapter 8, the final chapter, provides information and strategies for professional development, sustainment, and self-care strategies to remain competent *and* caring as a professional over the length of your career. The companion Web site for this text includes additional information.

Exercise: Exploring Losses in Your Own Life _____

Experiences with death or loss significantly influence the way we react to the losses of others, both consciously and unconsciously. It is important to recognize these experiences and how they might influence us in our daily work.

Take a few moments now to think about the following questions. You may want to write down your responses and reflect on them as you progress through the rest of this text, or use them as the beginning of a continuous journal.

- What was your earliest experience with death or loss? How old were you when it occurred? Where were you when you learned of the loss? Who did it involve? Describe what happened.
- What were the physical, emotional, and cognitive reactions you were aware of in yourself following this loss?
- How did the people around you respond to the loss? How did they respond to your reactions?
- How did your cultural and/or spiritual background influence your responses?
- What about the loss makes you feel vulnerable now?
- Based on what you have learned since, what do you think can help you to cope more easily with death or loss now and in the future?
- How do you think your own feelings and reactions to loss may impact your work with others who are experiencing loss or trauma?

If there are unresolved feelings about previous experiences with death or loss that you have not worked through it is important to find a way to address them so they do not negatively influence your work with others. Keeping a journal, joining support groups, participating in counseling, and even taking a course on grief can be helpful. There are many forums, chat rooms, and support groups available on the Internet that can be accessed through the links provided in this text. Choose the method that works best for you, but take the time you need to deal with your own losses. It will inevitably result in better care for others who are facing loss.

Self-Test

1. Professional competencies are important for which of the following reasons?
   a. They serve as an important self-assessment tool for professionals
   b. They inform the criteria for professional credentialing
   c. They are included in licensing examinations for professionals
   d. All of the above

2. What is secondary trauma?
   a. A reaction to the death of someone you only know distantly
   b. Trauma experienced by professionals working closely with those who have suffered from trauma
   c. A trauma reaction that surfaces six months after a traumatic event
   d. An anniversary reaction to a traumatic loss

3. Which of the following describes an interdisciplinary team?
   a. A team of professionals with a formal mechanism for communication and collaboration
   b. A team that consists of multiple professionals from different disciplines who do not necessarily have a formal mechanism for communication
   c. Two or more people in a school setting who are working to achieve student goals
   d. None of the above

Answers: 1) d   2) b   3) a

Internet Resources

Competency Standards Assessments and other instruments can be downloaded from the Toolkit for Change, published by Supportive Care of the Dying at http://www.careofdying.org

The Web site for Bill Moyers's PBS series, *On Our Own Terms,* with self-assessment tools and information, can be viewed at http://www.pbs.org/wnet/onourownterms/tools/index.html

The Center for Personal Recovery Web site includes publications on school and community responses to crisis and can be viewed at http://www.renew.net

The Association for Death Education and Counseling offers a variety of workshops, conferences, and continuing education programs related to death and grief at http://www.adec.org

The National Association of Social Workers Standards for Practice in End of Life Care can be found at http://www.naswdc.org

References

Brenner, P. (1999) When caregivers grieve. In K. Dota, *Living with grief: At work, at school, at worship* (pp. 81–92). Washington, D.C.: Hospice Foundation of America.

Furmanek, R. (2004). *Loss and bereavement journal.* Springfield, MA: Springfield College School of Social Work.

Hdlacki, R. (2004). *Loss and bereavement journal.* Springfield, MA: Springfield College School of Social Work.

Kirkland, R. (2003). *Loss and bereavement journal.* Springfield, MA: Springfield College School of Social Work.

Rando, T. (1984). *Grief, dying and death: Clinical interventions for caregivers.* Champaign, IL: Research Press Company.

Supportive Care of the Dying. (2004). Competency Standards/Assessment Tool. *Toolkit for change.* Retrieved on January 28, 2004 from http://www.careofdying.org.

Stonberg, M. (1980). *Listen with your heart.* Boston, MA: Boston Social Work Oncology Group.

Walker, J. (1997). *Feeling light in the dark.* Northampton, MA: Pioneer Valley Breast Cancer Network.

Ward, J. (2003). *Loss and bereavement journal.* Springfield, MA: Springfield College School of Social Work.

Worden, W. (2002). *Grief counseling and grief therapy: A handbook for the mental health practitioner.* (3rd ed.). New York: Springer Publishing.

3

Loss and Grief Across the Lifespan

Topics _____

Childhood

Adolescence

Young Adulthood

Middle Adulthood

Late Adulthood

Advanced Age

> *My story is about my mom. She had a disease. It was called leukemia. She had to go in the hospital for a long time. Then she came home. That was the best day. The worst day was when she had to go back in the hospital. I was crying when my dad told me. Then a month later, my dad said my mom was dying. I was crying and my dad was too.*
>
> —Child, age 8, speaking in a children's bereavement group

As discussed in Chapter 1, grief is experienced in reaction to many kinds of losses people experience over a lifetime, not only those resulting from death. Different authors use various definitions for the term **grief**, but it is generally used to describe the *emotional, psychological, and physical reactions to loss*. The term **mourning** also has different definitions, but Worden's (2002) definition is used in this text to describe the *process of grieving that an individual goes through in adapting to a loss*. The term **bereavement** is almost universally applied to describe *the state of having experienced a loss through the death of a significant person*. When President John F. Kennedy was assassinated, millions of people reacted with shock, sadness, and anger—the common emotions of grief. In a national day of mourning, all government offices were closed allowing the people affected by his death to attend his funeral mass or view it on television, which helped many to grasp the reality of his death and

29

express their grief. Everyone in the nation, along with his family, were considered to be bereaved, having experienced the loss of their president.

While grief experts acknowledge that grief is a reaction to many different kinds of losses, symbolic as well as physical, research does not yet adequately tell us how reactions to symbolic losses differ from reactions to death. Most of the empirical studies that inform our understanding of grief have examined reactions to death. These studies are helpful because they can guide us in understanding the grief reactions of people of different ages, cultural backgrounds, and developmental stages to loss. If we understand, for example, how seven-year-old children typically react to loss due to a loved one's death, we can be better prepared to support and assist them through their mourning process. It can also help us to anticipate the potential grief reactions of young children to symbolic losses such as parental divorce or placement in foster care.

The focus in this chapter is on the lifespan and how grief, as a reaction to death, is generally experienced and expressed by individuals at different stages of life. This information is based on empirical studies and theoretical frameworks addressing "normal grief." Specific grief theories and information about complicated grief is included in Chapter 4. In this chapter common reactions of children, teens, younger adults, and older adults to loss are reviewed along with suggestions for those of us who are in a position to help them cope. Learning how to help people cope with loss through death can also help you to be attuned and responsive to the grief related emotions and behaviors that are expressed in reaction to other types of losses.

Responses to death are influenced by many different factors in addition to age and developmental stage. Some of these factors include gender, cultural, and spiritual background, and an individual's relationship to the person who died. The more dependent a person is on the person who has died, for example, the more he or she will be affected by changes in roles and functioning that the loss imposes. An elderly spouse who has depended on their deceased spouse to manage the household may experience significant anxiety regarding their own well being in the face of their partner's death. The demands of coping with new tasks such as shopping, food preparation, cleaning, and paying bills add stress to the other natural emotional reactions such as sadness. Similarly, a spouse caring for young children or teens may become overwhelmed by the demands of single parenting after the death of his or her partner. A young child who is dependent on an adult for emotional and physical care will react to the loss of this care. Sometimes their reaction will occur gradually as the impact of the loss becomes more evident to the child.

If the relationship between two individuals was conflicted before the loss occurred, perhaps due to alcohol abuse or domestic violence, the grieving survivor may experience a complicated grief reaction. More information about the factors that influence complicated grief reactions will be discussed in Chapter 4. Cultural, spiritual, and gender influences are also discussed in Chapter 5. All of these influences are important to keep in mind when working with individuals at different stages of the life span.

Childhood

Some of the factors that influence a child's cognitive, emotional, and behavioral reactions to death, in addition to their chronological age, include earlier experiences with death, the reactions of adults and the other children around them, and the child's own unique personality and coping style.

> The child's opportunity to share his or her feelings and memories, the parent's ability to cope with stress, and the child's steady relationships with other adults are also other factors that may influence grief (National Cancer Institute, 2003).

While children do experience grief reactions, they may not show their feelings, or articulate them, as openly as adults. Young children, even those grieving the loss of a very significant person such as a parent, may not outwardly evidence their grief. They may throw themselves into activities unrelated to those the rest of the family is undertaking, engaging in play activities at the funeral home while other members of the family are crying. Adults in the family may interpret this to mean that the child doesn't really understand, or has gotten over the death. This behavior does not necessarily indicate that the child is not experiencing grief, however. Often, young children are less able to put their feelings into words the way that older children and adults can. Young children are also highly distractible and they transition easily from one thought or emotion to another. Sometimes this protects them from painful feelings or thoughts that are too overwhelming.

Because young children may not have the same acquisition of language as older children or adults, feelings or fears may be expressed through behaviors rather than words. School age children, who may have more language skills, but who also may be more sensitive to others' reactions, may not verbalize directly, but may express their feelings and thoughts through artwork, play, or somatic (physical) complaints. Understanding common reactions of children at different stages of development, and being attuned to expressions of these reactions, can prepare family members, teachers, and other helping professionals to assist them.

Children's grief and developmental stages

Children at different stages of development will understand death and express their grief differently. Common reactions based on empirical and clinical literature are described for each of these stages, although it is important to keep in mind that every individual is unique and therefore may react somewhat differently, based on a complex mix of influential factors including gender, culture, and spirituality.

Infants

Key developmental issues for infants and toddlers are dependency and attachment. At the earliest stage of development, very young children need to feel secure in the care of adults. They must develop trust that nurturing adults will provide consistent shelter, protection, and love in order to develop healthy attachments in future relationships. While very young children do not yet have the capacity to recognize death, they will react to the loss of a consistent caregiver. There are some developmental tasks they have not yet achieved that make it more difficult for them to understand and cope with loss.

Developmental factors

- Dependence on caregivers for all basic needs.
- Limited object constancy—the understanding that a person or object exists, even if not physically present.
- Limited ability to verbalize.
- Few coping strategies to regulate tension.

Understanding of death   Infants do not recognize death, but they do experience feelings of loss in reaction to separation that are part of developing an awareness of death.

Reactions to loss   Infants who have been separated from their mothers or primary caregivers may be sluggish, quiet, and unresponsive to a smile or a coo. They may undergo physical changes such as weight loss, be less active, and sleep less. They may also cry and appear inconsolable.

What can help?

- Maintaining normal routines of care giving and familiar surroundings.
- Providing a consistent caregiver who can give frequent and lengthy periods of love and attention, including holding and hugging.
- Providing consistent, gentle physical and verbal reassurance and comfort.
- Expressing confidence in the child and the world.

Ages 2–3 (toddlers)

Like infants, toddlers are also almost completely dependent on caregivers to provide for their basic needs, although they begin making attempts at mastery and independence. They show great variation in their cognitive and emotional development. While toddlers have begun to acquire language, their ability to comprehend and verbally express ideas and feelings is still quite limited. Young children often confuse death with sleep and may experience anxiety related to this confusion as early as age three. They may express distress through regression, often giving up previously acquired skills such as speaking clearly, toileting, and self-soothing at bedtime.

Developmental factors

- Ambivalence about independence.
- Increasing comprehension and articulation of language.

- Beginning mastery of motor and fine motor skills.
- Learning by mimicking and following the examples of others.

Understanding of death Children under three generally cannot cognitively understand death. They cannot differentiate a parent's absence for a short time from a long time. They can sense loss or change in something but they often cannot verbally explain or discuss it.

Reactions to loss Children under age three often express discomfort or insecurity through frequent crying or protest. They express distress or sadness through withdrawal, loss of interest in usual activities, and changes in eating and sleeping patterns. They may show regression through clinging or screaming when a caregiver tries to leave, evidencing increased dependence in activities of daily living.

What can help?

- Maintaining normal routines and familiar surroundings.
- Providing consistent caregivers who can give frequent and lengthy periods of love and attention including holding and hugging.
- Providing consistent, gentle physical and verbal reassurance and comfort.
- Providing simple, understandable verbal explanations for changes.
- Naming feelings expressed by the child and those the child observes being expressed by others, such as, "Daddy feels sad, that is why he is crying."

Ages 3–6

Children at this stage of development are still thinking concretely and may perceive death as a kind of sleep; the person is alive in the child's mind, but only in a limited way or in a distant place. The child cannot fully separate death from life. Their concerns may be focused on how the death directly affects them. The child's concept of death may also involve magical thinking. For example, the child may think that his or her thoughts can cause another person to become sick or die. Grieving children under five may have trouble eating, sleeping, and controlling bladder and bowel functions.

Developmental factors

- Developing a fuller mastery of language.
- Learning to read.
- Continuing to master fine motor and physical skills.
- Expressing feelings through art and play.
- Acquiring social skills through interactions and observing others.

Understanding of death Because they cannot quite comprehend the difference between life and death, children at this age may view the deceased person as continuing to live in a limited way. They may ask questions about the deceased (for example, how does the deceased eat, breathe, or play?). While young children may know that death occurs physically, they usually think it is temporary or reversible, not final.

Reactions to loss   Since children depend on parents and other adults to take care of them, a grieving child may wonder who will care for them or meet their needs after the death of an important person. They may be very anxious that something bad like death could happen to them or someone else upon whom they are dependent, such as a surviving parent. They may exhibit searching behaviors such as repeatedly viewing videotapes or photographs of the deceased loved one, or asking when and how the loved one might return.

What can help? (In addition to the strategies suggested for younger children.)

- Explaining death in simple and direct terms, including only as much detail as the child is able to understand.
- Answering a child's questions honestly and directly, making sure that the child understands the explanations provided.
- Reassuring children about their own security and explaining that they will continue to be loved and cared for (they often worry that their surviving parent or caregiver will go away).
- Encouraging mastery of age appropriate skills while allowing for regression.
- Expressing confidence in the child and the world.

Ages 6–9

Children in this age range are commonly very curious about death and may ask questions about what happens to one's body when a person dies. They are striving for mastery, and in their attempt to make sense of death, children may attribute responsibility for death to themselves or others. They may even believe they have magical powers, thinking they have actually caused or contributed to a death if they had thought bad things or misbehaved, and may view death as a punishment. Because they are striving for mastery and want to be involved in family decisions, children this age and older often benefit from being invited to contribute to memorial ceremonies or activities. If the child wants to attend the funeral, wake, or memorial service, he or she should be given, in advance, a full explanation of what to expect.

Developmental factors

- Relationships with peers and adults are important.
- Striving for mastery of information and tasks.
- Superego and a sense of responsibility are developing.
- Cognitively, they are still thinking concretely.

Understanding of death   Children's questions often indicate their efforts to understand death fully. For example, a child may ask, "I know uncle Bob died, but can he still see us up in heaven?" This may be a way of testing reality and also reflects the struggle to comprehend more abstract concepts.

Reactions to loss   Grieving children can become afraid of going to school or have difficulty concentrating, may behave aggressively, become overly concerned about their own health, or withdraw from others. With information and support most children are able to carry on activities of daily living with confidence and competence, however children at this age may regress emotionally and demonstrate separation anxiety or clinging. Boys sometimes become more aggressive (i.e., acting out in school), instead of directly expressing their sadness. Girls may become withdrawn or inattentive. Children may feel abandoned by both their deceased parent and their surviving parent if the surviving parent is grieving and unable to emotionally support the child.

What can help? (In addition to strategies suggested for younger children.)

- Discussions of death that include proper words, such as 'died' and 'death.' (Phrases such as "passed away", "he is sleeping", or "we lost him" can confuse children and lead to misunderstanding.)
- Providing opportunities for children to ask questions freely and to express their feelings directly or through creative activities.
- Providing reassurance that the child's thoughts, feelings, and behavior did not cause death.
- Reading aloud stories or books that deal with death and allowing the child to share their reactions or questions.
- Inviting children to share memories and participate in ceremonies or remembrance activities.

Ages 9–12

This is a stage of intense exploration and mastery in physical, cognitive, social, emotional, and spiritual development. The child is developing an increasing grasp of abstract concepts and is learning about living systems in school. By the time a child is twelve years old death is seen as final and something that happens to everyone. Cultural and spiritual beliefs of the family and community are influential. In American society, for example, many adults avoid discussion of death or feelings of grief. Those who are grieving may withdraw rather than talk to others. Children, however, often talk to the people around them (even strangers) to see the reactions of others and to get clues for their own responses.

Developmental factors

- Interest in and capacity to understand biological processes.
- Heightened sensitivity to others' emotions (i.e., guilt, anger, shame).

- Increased awareness of vulnerability.
- Regressive and impulsive behaviors indicate stress.
- Prepubertal changes.

Understanding of death   By the time a child is nine years old, death is usually known to be unavoidable and is not seen as a punishment. Children may see death as final and frightening but may also see it as something that happens mostly to old people (and not to themselves or someone younger).

Reactions to loss   Children's reactions to death often reflect what they have learned from parents and other adults around them. The family's spiritual beliefs are often evident in the child's statements about death and coping. Although most bereaved children do not show serious emotional or behavioral disturbances, children who lose a loved one are at a greater risk for symptoms of depression, withdrawal, anxiety, conduct problems, changes in school performance, and low self-esteem. They are also capable of empathy and expressing caring to others who are grieving or who share similar experiences.

What can help?

- Talking about death can help children learn effective ways to cope with loss.
- Providing an opportunity to explore and discuss spiritual and cultural beliefs related to loss.
- Providing physical outlets for strong emotions.
- Encouraging expression of feelings through different media including art, music, dance, and writing.
- Letting children know they are not alone and that others experience loss and the feelings related to it.
- Modeling direct and constructive expression of feelings naturally associated with loss such as anger and sadness.

Adolescence

Adolescence is generally thought of as a time of intense change in biological, psychological, and social development. Most adolescents want to fit in with their peers and may view a death in the family as making them appear different from their peers, or they may perceive that the death has placed greater demands on their own developmental tasks such as career planning, exploring intimate relationships with partners, and achieving personal goals in school, athletics, or other activities. They may also be acutely aware of the discomfort others evidence in talking about death and modulate their reactions accordingly. All of these internal and external factors can lead teens to feel alienated or isolated from those who don't seem to understand.

Developmental factors

- Searching for identity.
- Exploring sex and intimacy.
- Peer relationships are very important.
- Exposure to maladaptive responses to stress.
- Abstract thinking.

Understanding of death Adolescents comprehend that death is permanent, irreversible, and affects everyone. While they cognitively understand that death is final and inevitable, their behavior may indicate denial.

Reactions to loss Adolescents are capable of mature and thoughtful reflections on the meaning of life and death and may struggle with existential questions. Grieving adolescents are at risk for exposure to maladaptive coping strategies such as substance abuse, risk-taking, and sexual experimentation. They are also exposed to media influences that have destructive themes and uncensored violence (Leming, 2002). They may also be at risk for parentification—taking on adult roles and tasks before they are developmentally ready.

What can help?

- Talking openly about death, indicating that the subject is not off-limits.
- Verbal or written explanations that tears, sadness, anger, guilt, and confusion are all part of normal grief.
- Providing opportunities for adolescents to hear from and talk with peers who have also experienced loss. (Bereavement groups and retreats can be very effective.)
- Inviting the adolescent to help plan or participate in memorial or remembrance activities in the way that feels most comfortable to them.
- Connecting adolescents to peers who have similar experiences to reduce isolation. This can be done through facilitated Internet discussions or Web sites.
- Encouraging keeping a journal or using other methods to express thoughts and feelings.
- Constructing memorials, memory books, boxes, or quilts, or providing other tangible ways to memorialize significant relationships.

Young Adulthood

Young adulthood is one of the most exciting and challenging periods in a person's life. Major decisions about job and career choices, choosing a partner, and bearing and raising children are being made, and this may be the first time in their life that they have true responsibilities to others. Moral decisions also come into play during this developmental phase. Many young adults facing loss—their own as well as others'—may struggle with a sense of obligation to self and others. A major strength at this age is that they have had exposure to a wide variety of coping strategies and are often open to learning new ones. While fully capable of understanding death and its impact, the multiple demands of life may deter their ability to devote time and energy to grief.

Developmental factors

- Expected to be self-sufficient (economically, if not emotionally).
- Developing career and life plans.
- Establishing partnerships or a family of their own.
- Expanding their range of roles and coping strategies.

Understanding of death   When young people reach adult status, they fully comprehend the impact of death—both the immediate impact for the deceased and the long–term impact for survivors. Young adults are also capable of comprehending the complex range of responses of different people to different types of losses.

Reactions to loss   Young adults may struggle with their feelings of responsibility for other family members after a loss and may be ambivalent about meeting their own needs or the needs of others. They may perceive tears and sadness as indicating weakness, or evidence guilt about their own actions or inactions related to the death. Young adults are also vulnerable to the emergence of anxiety, depression, and other disorders that stress related to loss can exacerbate.

What can help?

- Acknowledging the multiple impacts of loss and the normalcy of grief reactions.
- Encouraging individuals to take time to attend to their own feelings as well as those of others.
- Acknowledging or providing opportunities for expression and discussion of conflicting feelings.
- Promoting social connections through peer support and group activities.
- Referring young adults to credible Internet sources for information and peer support.

Middle Adulthood

Sometimes referred to as the "sandwich" generation, middle-aged adults are meeting multiple obligations in work, family, and community. They may be involved in raising children, or later in this life stage "launching" their young-adult children. The role of parent brings with it many responsibilities as well as complex feelings related to losses and gains. At the same time, middle-aged adults may be called upon to assist their own parents or older family members, whose frailty can raise existential questions as well as serve as a reminder of their own vulnerability. Relationships are complex, and those that are conflicted may result in complicated grief reactions when they end. Seeking meaning and satisfaction, many middle-aged adults are leaders or major contributors in their families, work settings, and community organizations. Biological changes are occurring in both men and women that influence mood and physical capacities.

Developmental factors

- Re-examination, renewal, and/or reintegration of identity.
- Multiple roles and responsibilities.
- Long-established patterns may be difficult to change (e.g., substance dependence).
- Increased vulnerability to physical disorders (e.g., cancer, heart disease).

Reactions to loss   Middle adults may experience a "pile-up" of losses, related to deaths and other life-changing events. Divorces, adult children moving to distant locations, and more deaths among their friends and family members often occur in mid-life. Maladaptive patterns, such as the use of substances and avoidance of painful feelings or intimacy through work, may make the process of grieving complicated. Fully aware of the impact of death and the existential questions it raises, mid-life adults may also experience increased sensitivity and openness to others and alternative ways of coping. This generative stage of development often means that satisfaction is derived from helping others or making contributions to one's community. Religious or spiritual practices are often comforting. Grieving the loss of a child or a long-term marriage can be particularly painful and protracted.

What can help? (In addition to those strategies recommended for younger adults.)

- Empathic listening and support.
- Release time from work or school to meet family obligations and process grief.
- Bereavement support groups.
- Tangible expressions of support or caring such as preparing meals or assisting with the care of children or elder family members.
- Pastoral care or connection with a religious or spiritual community.
- Identification of risk factors and offering intervention for complicated grief.
- Opportunities for respite and renewal.
- Opportunities to assist others, when interest in this is expressed.

Late Adulthood

In general, in American society, when an adult reaches age 65 he or she is considered an older adult, although many people this age do not consider themselves old, and the terms 'old age' and 'elder' may be perceived as negative. The impacts of many physical, social, and economic changes at this stage of development are compounded and loss is highly likely to become a more routine part of life. Many adults in this stage desire to leave a legacy through future generations, accomplishments, or possessions. Life can be viewed in a historical context, and life review becomes an important activity.

Developmental factors

- Poor health or disabling medical conditions may have significant impact as biological aging progresses.
- Serenity and wisdom may be sought.
- Changes in identity related to work and family occur.
- Adaptation to changes in information processing and memory is required to maintain maximum functioning.

Reactions to loss   Multiple losses require continuing adaptation. If significant family members or friends die, individuals must adjust to the new environment in which those persons are no longer present. If retirement or changes in roles and responsibilities due to illness or aging are unwanted or forced, grief reactions may be intense and maladaptive. Isolation and limited social support may contribute to adjustment problems, and changes in economic status, particularly for widowed women, can contribute to increased stress. It may be difficult to differentiate between grief and depression, particularly when multiple biological, psychological, and social changes are occurring in the face of multiple losses.

What can help?

- Acknowledgment of symbolic losses as well as losses through death.
- Maintaining or augmenting social supports.
- Provision of income supports or economic assistance, when needed.
- Conducting informal and formal life review, with emphasis on strengths and contributions.
- Identifying new activities, roles, and relationships to augment or replace those that have been lost.

Advanced Age

An increasing number of adults are living to the age of 80 and older. While many are physically capable of carrying out work, creative projects, and activities of daily living independently, eventually everyone in this age group faces death—their own as well as the deaths of partners, other family members, and friends. A large number of these oldest adults are frail and experience chronically disabling illnesses and medical conditions. Memory impairment and other mental disorders increase with age. Social isolation often increases as mobility decreases and social support networks diminish. Placement in long-term care increases as well, and elders must often adjust not only to multiple caregivers but also multiple changes in caregivers. These changes represent many symbolic losses in addition to the multiple deaths already experienced by this stage in life.

Developmental factors

* Vulnerability to social isolation, disabling medical conditions, and memory loss.
* Adaptation to multiple losses, both symbolic and through deaths.
* Change in sense of time.
* A sense of consummation and conclusion in life.

Reactions to loss   At this stage of life, most individuals begin to anticipate their own death, at some point in the near or not-too-distant future at the same time that they are grieving or adapting to other losses. Deaths of significant others may have a serious impact on social support, particularly if one's social support network has diminished. Acceptance of death may be more prevalent than anger. Reminiscence is a common activity and often brings a positive sense of closure and fulfillment to adults of advanced age.

What can help?

* Reminiscence through sharing of memories, with individuals and groups.
* Providing concrete supports to allow expenditure of time and energy on satisfying activities and relationships such as helping with household maintenance or bill paying.
* Acknowledging losses as well as strengths and coping capacities.
* Encouraging completion of advance directives such as living wills, durable powers of attorney, and health care proxy directions.
* Providing opportunities to openly discuss ideas, values, feelings, and fears related to dying and death.

Exercise: Grief Reactions at Different Stages of Life _____

The Internet is the fastest growing source of information about grief. To test this you can type the keyword 'grief' into your favorite search engine. (More than 3 million hits were identified in my recent search.) It is difficult to know which sources of information are the most credible and helpful. In the Internet Resources for this chapter you will find selected Web sites that are used frequently by both professionals and consumers. To learn more about grief reactions at different stages of life and about what information is available, try the following activity.

- Create your own archive or database of useful Web sites and articles that address grief and loss. You may want to create a system for saving information into topic areas such as Children's Grief, Teen Loss, Pet Loss, etc. You can use a bookmark function on your computer, save the information to a hard drive or disk, or use an archiving program or Web site.
  - If you are completing this activity as part of a classroom exercise, you can divide into small groups, with each member taking responsibility for researching and archiving information on a specific grief-related topic. You can then compile your information to share with the entire class.
  - Begin by visiting the links listed in the Internet Resources for this chapter. Read the information posted on a given topic at each of the sites. Compare the similarities and differences in the information provided.
  - Discuss with your classmates or a grief expert which sites they have found most useful and why.
  - Save your file or database and add to it as you continue your career development.

Self-Test

1. At which stage of development are children generally thought to understand the finality of death?
   a. Ages 3-6
   b. Ages 6-9
   c. Ages 9-12
   d. Adolescence

2. Why are bereavement support groups helpful for adolescents?
   a. Peer relationships are important to adolescents and groups reduce the sense of isolation that bereaved teens can experience
   b. Adults cannot understand adolescents' feelings related to loss
   c. Adolescents have not acquired effective strategies to cope with stress
   d. Individual counseling does not work with adolescents

   Answers: 1) c 2) a

Internet Resources

The National Cancer Institute provides information about grief reactions at different ages at http://www.cancer.gov/cancerinfo/pdq/supportivecare/bereavement/patient/

The Children's Hospital of Iowa hosts a virtual children's hospital with articles on topics including children's grief at http://www.vh.org/pediatric/patient/pediatrics/cqqa/grief.html

There are many commercial and non-profit Internet sites that offer information and support to people of all ages who are grieving. Some of these are constructed by grief experts and some are not. Examples of commercial sites include: http://beyondindigo.com and http://www.journeyofhearts.org/jofh/grief/help2

Both the Hospice Foundation of America and the National Hospice and Palliative Care Organization are excellent sources of information about grief and the resources that may be available through your community hospice programs. (http://www.hospicefoundation.org/griefandloss/ and http://www.nhpco.org)

There are many organizations to support grieving children and their families that post information on their Web sites. Examples of these include: http://www.dougy.org and http://www.thefrontporch.org

Compassionate Friends is an organization supporting parents who have experienced the death of a child. Their Web site is http://www.compassionatefriends.org

The American Association of Retired Persons (AARP) offers information, programs, and services related to grief and loss at http://www.aarp.org/griefandloss/

The National Cancer Institute offers information for both consumers and professionals, respectively, at: http://www.nci.nih.gov/cancertopics/pdg/supportivecare/bereavement/ patient and http://www.nci.nih.gov/cancertopics/pdg/supportivecare/bereavement/ healthprofessional/page8/

References

Leming, M., & Dickinson, G. (2002). *Understanding dying, death, and bereavement.* (5th ed.). New York: Harcourt College Publishers.

National Cancer Institute. (2003). Retrieved on January 8, 2005 from http://www.cancer.gov/cancerinfo/ pdq/supportivecare/bereavement/patient/

Worden, W. (2002). *Grief counseling and grief therapy: A handbook for the mental health practitioner.* (3rd ed.). New York: Springer Publishing Company.

4

Normal and Complicated Grief Reactions

> *And can it be that in a world so full and busy the loss of one creature*
> *makes a void in any heart so wide and deep that nothing but the width*
> *and depth of eternity can fill it up!*
>
> —Charles Dickens

One of the most common questions grieving people ask is, "Is this reaction normal?"
This same question is also asked by many professionals who are attempting to determine when, and if, an individual might need specialized help in order to cope with
a loss.

Case Example

Mike and his sister, Mary, both work in a large corporation in the community where
they were raised. Mary has called the human resources department asking for a referral
to the EAP (Employee Assistance Program) because of her concern about Mike. She
thinks Mike may need help because he is still showing signs of depression since his wife
died two and a half years ago. Prior to his wife's death, he socialized a great deal. He
has since isolated himself and abandoned activities that used to interest him such as golf,

gardening, and going out after work with his buddies or his siblings once or twice a week. Since the death of his wife he has not made any changes to anything that belonged to her, including their bedroom where her clothing still hangs in the closet. Mike hired a neighborhood boy to cut the lawn and make minor repairs on the house—activities that Mike used to enjoy. The inside of the house has become uncharacteristically untidy. Mary has visited repeatedly and offered to help clean, but Mike has resisted her help and given her instructions not to eliminate anything that reminds him of his wife, including giving away or storing her knick-knacks, aprons, or clothes. He also visits the cemetery every Sunday rather than participating in routine family gatherings or even special events. Mary is concerned that her brother is depressed. She says that he had a strong reaction when their father died during their college years. Mike had met his wife shortly before his father's death and had married her relatively soon after. Mary is seeking advice about whether he might need to see a counselor and how she can best help him.

Theories That Inform Our Understanding of Grief

Our understanding of normal or expectable grief reactions comes from many sources. Over the past half-century, many theories have been constructed to explain human attachment and the grief reactions that result from loss. Some theories have been constructed by researchers studying large groups of grieving people. Other theories have been constructed by psychiatrists, psychologists, and other mental health professionals who provide treatment to grieving individuals. While these theories are useful, they all have the potential for cultural bias, as they have been constructed by individuals who have lived and studied in a particular location at a particular time in history. While it is clear that grief is a universal human reaction, it is not clear that each theory can be universally applied to all people, in all cultures and time periods.

Many reactions that are considered a natural part of a culturally prescribed grief reaction in one cultural group may seem highly unusual, even distressing, to members of another cultural group. Therefore, before addressing the topic of normal and complicated grief it is important to note that culture is a very significant influence in the way that people express their grief, just as it is an influence in the way that people deal with most other life situations. The topics of culture and spirituality are explored in more depth in Chapter 5, but it is important to recognize that each individual may express their grief uniquely and it is always wise to reserve judgment until we understand the cultural context of behavior. The information in Chapter 5 will help to prepare you for culturally sensitive practice. However, the information that has been gathered by researchers and grief therapists and the theories they have constructed can help guide us in understanding and helping people who are grieving. A brief overview of some key theories and theorists is important in order to understand how the concepts of normal and complicated grief are applied.

Sigmund Freud was one of the first psychiatrists credited with contributing to the theoretical understanding of grief. His basic ideas were written in *Mourning and Melancholia,* first published in 1917. Subsequent theorists have elaborated on, and even disagreed with, what Freud wrote, but his work still informs many grief therapists. Freud theorized that every human infant develops attachments to significant people (who he referred to as "objects") through the process of cathexis. **Cathexis** refers to the *process of attaching emotionally* and is crucial to healthy development since it is through attachments with others that the infant learns to trust that basic needs (food, protection, and love) will be met. Freud also identified the process of **decathexis**, or the *process of letting go of an attachment as an adaptive response to loss of a significant "object" (person).* The process involves both intellectually and emotionally releasing the attachment.

John Bowlby is another important theorist who elaborated on the ideas that Freud developed about human attachment and loss. Bowlby (1973) proposed that attachment behavior toward caregivers in human infants helps them establish and maintain a sense of security throughout their life. He observed that infants and children react with searching behaviors when separated from a significant person (in his era defined most often as the mother) in an attempt to reestablish the bond and sense of security that the presence of the caregiver provides. According to Bowlby's theory, the grief reaction of the bereaved to the loss of a significant other is a similar process. The bereaved must cease investing their emotional energy (referred to as libido by both Freud and Bowlby) in the deceased in order to reinvest it in other relationships. Bowlby noted that, just like the infant who continues to search for the significant other, a grieving individual may try to avoid or deny the reality of separation that death imposes. Even when the reality of the loss is acknowledged intellectually, the grieving person continues for a period of time to maintain an emotional connection with the deceased. Anger and sadness, along with a sense of emptiness, are all part of the normal, expected reactions that those who have suffered the loss of a significant person experience. Both Freud and Bowlby believed that with the passage of time grieving individuals could—on their own or with help—both intellectually and emotionally achieve decathexis, or withdraw energy (libido) from the deceased. Failure to eventually do this—to free oneself from the clinging attachment—they believed, resulted in emotional or psychological difficulty, often described as depression. Many grief experts still use these basic concepts to explain why mourning is considered a normal process in reaction to loss.

Eric Lindemann (1944), conducted research that supported much of what Freud and Bowlby had written about grief. Lindemann became very interested in studying grief reactions after a major tragedy in Boston, the Coconut Grove nightclub fire, took the lives of 492 people. Many of the victims were college students celebrating the football victory of Holy Cross College over Boston College in the over-crowded night club in November of 1942. Lindeman studied the grieving survivors to learn more about how people react to the death of a significant other. He found that common reactions in the acute period following the death included physical or bodily distress, preoccupation with the image of the person who had died, anger or hostility, guilt, and impaired functioning in work or family roles. He also identified tasks that grievers appeared to complete that resulted in a diminishment of these symptoms. The tasks included acknowledging the reality of the death, adjusting to life without the deceased person, and forming new relationships. Lindemann's task model has informed later grief theorists as well as therapists.

The person whose name is most closely linked with the topic of grief in many people's minds is Elizabeth Kubler-Ross, a physician who worked extensively with dying patients. Kubler-Ross (1997) made major contributions to our understanding of **anticipatory grief**, *the reactions of people who are dying*, in her pioneering publications in the 1960s and 1970s that described her stage model of adjustment to death. She proposed that people who have been told they will die from a terminal illness go through five stages:

1. Denial
2. Bargaining
3. Anger
4. Sadness
5. Acceptance

Many subsequent writers and practitioners have applied the Kubler-Ross model to those who are grieving, suggesting that individuals who are grieving the death of a significant other also experience the reactions that Kubler-Ross described in patients who are dying. It is important to note, however, that many contemporary practitioners question Kubler-Ross's stage model, noting that not all patients diagnosed with life-limiting illness evidence all five stages, and if they do, they do not always move through them sequentially. Other practitioners note that Kubler-Ross's model was constructed based on work with individuals who were actually dying, not those grieving the death of someone else.

More recently, grief counselors such as Therese Rando (1984, 1993) and William Worden (2002) have expanded on earlier theories in order to provide practical guidance to professionals working with those who are grieving. Rando, a grief counselor who has authored many books on grief and loss, suggests that many clients who seek psychotherapy for problems such as depression or anxiety often present issues of unresolved loss, either symbolic or actual. They may not seek help until years after the loss and may not recognize that their distress is related to grief. She and many other mental health specialists suggest that a wide variety of losses, not just the death of a loved one, can precipitate a grief reaction. Symbolic losses, discussed in Chapter 1, may include the loss of the family life when divorce occurs, the loss of the type of future one imagined for a child if the child is born with, or acquires, a disabling condition, and the symbolic loss of one's biological family after adoption. It is useful to remember that acknowledgment and support of an individual or family are important in helping them to cope with both loss through death *and* symbolic losses.

Common Reactions in Normal Grief

Normal grief

Information that grief experts have accumulated about "normal" or typical reactions to loss in individuals at different stages of development was presented in Chapter 3. It is now well recognized that individuals manifest a wide spectrum of grief reactions that also vary according to cultural backgrounds, social support networks, gender, socioeconomic status, as well as psychological health and the circumstances of loss. A very happily married older man who enjoys solid social support and many activities may express feelings and behave very differently after the death of his spouse than an older woman who has financial worries, few social supports, and who had a conflicted marriage. Both may experience normal grief. Like many people who experience a significant loss and normal grief, they may cope effectively and will not require mental health or grief intervention. Most often, the social and emotional support that is provided by friends, families and communities assists the grieving individual or family, helping them through acknowledging their loss, sharing the pain, and supporting their adjustment to the new situation. Children, adolescents, and adults all benefit from this kind of social, emotional, and practical support.

It is important to understand the wide range of behaviors that are considered to be a part of normal grieving because grieving individuals may experience them as frightening or disturbing and need reassurance that these are part of an expectable reaction.

- Sadness, anger, guilt, anxiety, loneliness, fatigue, helplessness, numbness, shock and even relief (in cases such as the prolonged illness of a loved one or the end of a conflicted relationship) are all feelings that are normal and expectable following a significant loss.
- Tightness in the chest or throat, lack of energy, and stomach distress are physical (or somatic) sensations that are common in response to loss.
- Confusion, inability to concentrate or remember details, and auditory or visual experiences that mimic hallucinations—such as seeing an image of the deceased person or hearing their voice—are not uncommon in the weeks or months following loss.
- Sleep disturbance, loss of appetite, and restlessness are also very common reactions.

Over the course of time, with adequate social support and the opportunity to participate in grieving rituals within a cultural or spiritual community, most individuals will gradually experience a diminishment of these feelings, behaviors, and sensations. Grief experts are often asked if there is a normal expectable timeframe within which acute grief will be resolved. Rather than trying to assess a griever's needs based on the time period that has passed after a loss, it is generally more helpful to assess how intensely the distress is experienced and how much it interferes with the grieving individual or family's ability to resume important activities and participate in other relationships after the loss. If an individual or members of a family continue to experience distress intensely or for a prolonged period—or even years after a loss—they may be experiencing a complicated grief reaction and could benefit from treatment for complicated grief.

Complicated Grief

In some situations an individual may have *difficulty coping with loss and* have *prolonged distress long after the loss has occurred.* This can occur even when environmental or social support has been strong. It is important to be attuned to this reaction, often described as **complicated grief** or **complicated mourning**, because counseling may help the grieving individual or family to work through the painful feelings of loss.

Drawing from Bowlby, Lindemann, and Rando's work as well as his own research, Worden (2002) has identified four tasks that he considers a necessary part of the mourning process. These tasks include:

1. Acceptance of the loss.
2. Experiencing the pain of grief.
3. Adjusting to the new environment without the deceased.
4. Relocating and memorializing the loved one (p. 47).

Worden emphasizes that these tasks must be completed in order for an individual to adapt to the loss of a significant other. Failure to eventually complete these tasks, according to his model, results in several types of complicated mourning. **Delayed grief** occurs *when a loss is insufficiently mourned,* often because the loss is not acknowledged or the grief is not supported by others. The delayed grief then appears later in the individual's life. *When grief is absent immediately after a loss but appears later in the form of a medical or psychiatric problem,* it is referred to as **masked grief**. *When a normal grief reaction, such as depressed mood or anxiousness, goes beyond normal grief to a clinical level of depression or anxiety,* it is referred to as **exaggerated grief**. **Chronic grief** is *when the mourner is stuck, sometimes for many years, in the grief process.* Worden recommends grief therapy for all types of complicated grief.

Who is at risk for complicated grief?

There are many factors that influence how grieving individuals cope with loss and that may contribute to complicated grief reactions. Individuals and families experiencing complicated grief will be encountered in many different settings, so it is important to be familiar with risk factors.

Circumstances surrounding a loss **Disenfranchised losses** are *losses accompanied by stigma resulting in loss of support or acknowledgment for grieving survivors.* The execution of a prisoner, losses associated with AIDS, and the death of a drunk driver following a fatal accident are examples of these types of losses. Many people close to a person who has died by suicide feel a complex mix of guilt and isolation that can make acknowledgment and acceptance of the loss more complicated. Grieving family members sometimes hope to avoid stigma so they may not let others know of their loss or feelings about it. Sometimes the loss is not acknowledged by others who could provide support, because they are unsure about how to express their condolences. Many adoption and foster care workers as well as graduates of the foster care system report that the symbolic loss inherent in removal from one's biological family precipitates a grief reaction that is not sufficiently acknowledged or formally addressed in the formal child welfare system. Grieving loved ones experiencing disenfranchised grief may carry their complicated and unacknowledged feelings for many years.

Some losses are so unique that they can be expected to produce intense grief reactions for a very long time, even when there is adequate support for grief following the loss. Among these is the death of a child. A child's death is outside of the normal sequence of life events. Parents expect their children to outlive them and to carry on the family heritage. Research indicates that the grief of parents for a deceased child is particularly severe when compared with other types of bereavement (Rando, 1984). For parents, the process of mourning for a child involves not only dealing with the loss of the child, but with the symbolic loss of parts of oneself, since parental attachment consists of both love for the child and self-love. The mourning process also may involve a perceived loss or lessening of social support.

Many parents whose children have died report that others do not know how to support them in this unique type of loss and thus may avoid the grieving parents or avoid discussing their painful feelings with them. This can result in a sense of social isolation that can magnify the loss.

Dale Link offers a parent's perspective on this experience. Dale and her husband Gerry lost two of their children to cystic fibrosis. Their daughter Bonnie was diagnosed with the disease in 1976 at six months of age. In caring for Bonnie they met other people affected by the disease. One very special person they came to know was a little boy named David. David had been abandoned by his parents and was a ward of the state. Dale and Gerry were so touched by David that they opened their home and hearts and adopted him when he was still a baby. They were able to share many special times together as a family with Bonnie, David, and their oldest son Michael, who was spared from the genetic disease. David lived to the age of six before he passed away. Four years later Bonnie passed away at age seventeen. It was an extremely difficult time for Dale and her family. "I felt as though I was majoring in grief and dying without a textbook for what to do," she said. Even though Dale had been working as a registered nurse and had seen many people die, she was not at all prepared for dealing with her own grief. Mostly she remembers feeling very isolated and alone. She knew people cared yet they seemed uncomfortable, not knowing what to do or say. Rather than risking a mistake, they often just stayed away. Friends who had children later shared with her that they did not want to come around because of their own guilt in having healthy children. They thought it would be too hard for her to be with them. Dale says, "Looking back it is more clear to me than ever that as a society we do not know how to cope with death. It is ironic that at a time when people need each other the most, they often feel the most alone'" (Schraffenberger, 2000).

Parents whose children have been removed from their care by protective service organizations, or who have relinquished the role of parent through adoption, experience grief that is often intensified by shame, guilt, and isolation. Yet support is rarely provided to assist with this grief. Strategies for assisting high-risk individuals and families will be discussed at the end of this chapter, and in later chapters. In the case of parents whose children have died, as well as other situations in which social isolation complicates grief such as loss from suicide, peer support can be most helpful and can be enhanced through referral to a grieving parents' support group or a program that addresses these specific types of losses.

Case Example

Chereen and Mike are parents whose only child, Kyle, died unexpectedly from meningitis while attending college. Although equally devastated, they were coping differently with the loss, and strain had developed in their marriage. Mike mostly expressed anger and guilt, questioning the medical procedures that led to the late diagnosis and treatment and isolating himself from friends and family. Chereen more frequently expressed intense sadness. She cried openly and talked frequently about Kyle with family and friends, finding comfort in being with her extended family including a nephew and several nieces. Chereen's co-workers in a local real estate office were concerned as they listened to her worry about Mike's anger and his tendency toward isolation. Mike's co-workers in an elementary school were concerned because he seemed withdrawn, didn't speak about Kyle, and they felt uncomfortable approaching him. Through a notice posted in the school's parent newsletter, Mike read about a group meeting for parents who had lost a child, sponsored by an organization called Compassionate Friends. Although he wasn't eager to attend any group, he and Chereen agreed that this group might be a place to meet people who really understood what it was like for them. In the first group meeting, Mike and Chereen heard from other parents that their reactions were common and were understood by others in the group. Other couples spoke about how, as individuals, they grieved differently too, and sometimes felt isolated from family and friends who had not lost a child. They also talked about ways they had found to gain sustenance from each other, even though the pain was intense. Mike and Chereen were surprised to hear that other parents had found a way to gain meaning and even some hope, even though they all had experienced a devastating tragedy. They attended the group regularly for about a year and became active supporters of other couples whose young adult children had died.

Perceived lack of social support   Other types of losses can result in a difficult mourning process, partly because of a perceived or actual lack of social support. Suicide, as noted previously, is a difficult loss to sustain because of the social stigma associated with it, and because survivors often perceive a lack of social support. Older adults who have already sustained the loss of many members of their primary support network—including friends, siblings, and adult children—may have limited social support to help them adjust and to fill the void when someone important in their life dies. An example of such a situation is the nursing home resident whose roommate dies. Partners in gay and lesbian relationships, especially among elders whose relationships may not be publicly acknowledged, report feeling isolated when their relationships end in a way that heterosexual partners may not. Often, symbolic losses are not acknowledged in the way that loss from death is acknowledged. Since there are no pre-established shared public rituals to assist the individual or family that has sustained a symbolic loss, such as loss sustained through divorce or placement in foster care, there may be no formal way for the difficult feelings of sadness or anger to be acknowledged or for support to be provided.

David Pelzar (1997) describes the complicated feelings of a child placed in foster care in his best-selling book *The Lost Boy*. Removed from his mother's care due to horrific abuse and placed in several different foster homes, the child's behavior became increasingly problematic and he expressed self-blame, sadness, and anger. He displayed searching behaviors when he secretly rode his bicycle past his biological family's home after he had been refused contact with his mother or siblings. When asked what he was looking for he answered, "I don't understand why I'm not allowed to see or talk to her or the boys. What did I do? I just want to know . . . why things happened like they did" (p. 165). In reading this and other accounts of children in foster care it is clear that helping systems have not yet adequately addressed the grief reactions of this vulnerable population.

When an individual experiences perceived or actual lack of social support after a loss, professionals can provide much needed support through active listening as well as referrals to support groups and organizations that provide information and peer exchange. More about these strategies will be discussed at the conclusion of this chapter as well as in Chapter 6.

High profile losses   Lack of social support is not a problem in some very high profile losses. Instead, in these cases, intense media coverage and public attention may overwhelm members of a family or community. Many survivors of the terrorist attacks of 9/11 and of public losses such as a police officer's death in the line of duty have acknowledged that lack of privacy and frequent inquiries about, or exposure to, the details of the loss make it difficult to obtain needed respite. Prolonged and intensified grief can result when graphic details of the death are repeatedly encountered by survivors who are often subjected to insensitive reporting and unrelenting public exposure. Some survivors and trauma specialists believe that it can actually add to survivors' distress when too much attention is focused on the loss, particularly the traumatic details, or when survivors are urged to talk about the trauma repeatedly (Cambell, 2002). Some survivors of very public tragedies report that distress is relieved more successfully through taking action, such as forming task groups to influence policy or obtaining resources for survivor families and communities. In situations of complicated grief that can result from high profile tragedies, however, peer support and professionally led programs are reported to be very helpful (Kirby, 1999).

Multiple stressors   Unfortunately, many losses are accompanied by additional stressors such as reduced income or unexpected financial debt, loss of important roles, or even the loss of a job or health insurance. Single parenting is often an additional stressor in situations where an active partner in parenting dies or leaves the family. It is important for professionals to be aware that these factors will often intensify the grief reaction or make it more difficult for individuals to complete the necessary tasks of grieving, since they may be preoccupied by these additional challenges and unable to achieve relief from the pain of loss. When learning that someone has sustained a loss, professionals can be attuned to the additional strains the grieving person may be experiencing and inquire about these so needed help can be obtained.

It is also important to be familiar with factors that might predict if an individual or a family is at risk for complicated bereavement if you are working with them during a serious or chronic illness. A study by Kelly et al. (1999) looked at predictors of bereavement outcome among family caregivers of cancer patients. They discovered that families with the greatest distress in bereavement had suffered a greater number of adverse life events, had prior losses or separations in their lives, and had more troubled relationships with the patient. Kelly also discovered that the patient was more severely ill at the time of palliative care referral. Further, being psychologically distressed prior to the patient's death predicted greater distress for the family caregiver following the death.

Kissane et al. (1998) classified five types of family responses to a death and labeled maladaptive responses as those involving hostile or sullen reactions, which were characterized by high family conflict, low expressiveness, and poor expressiveness. The researchers used a 12-item Family Relationships Index (Moos, 1981) and found it to be an effective screening tool to identify families at risk. Awareness of risk factors can enable professionals to make appropriate referrals for support prior to or following a death and, perhaps, ameliorate complicated grief.

Interventions for Normal and Complicated Grief

Why and how can a referral to a mental health professional or grief therapist help?

Mental health professionals include social workers, psychologists, psychiatrists, pastoral care, and other counselors. These professionals are trained to assess individuals' mental health and emotional distress. The primary tool used to guide the mental health assessment is the Diagnostic and Statistical Manual of Mental Disorders (DSM-IV) published by the American Psychiatric Association (2000). The manual provides guidelines to make an accurate assessment of symptoms that may be indicative of uncomplicated bereavement or a more serious depression. The DSM-IV manual notes that some depressive symptoms are a normal and expectable reaction to the death of a loved one. These symptoms, including sadness, diminished interest in daily activities, weight loss, and diminished ability to concentrate, may all be evident in uncomplicated bereavement, which is not classified as a mental disorder. As noted above, people are usually able to cope with loss and grief with the support of family, friends, and often a spiritual community. However, when risk factors are present or when individuals are evidencing signs of complicated bereavement, the individual may require specialized grief intervention. According to the DSM-IV, bereavement is considered to be complicated by a major depressive episode *if* the depressive symptoms (sadness, weight loss, diminished ability to concentrate) are accompanied by morbid preoccupation with worthlessness, suicidal ideation, and/or marked functional impairment or psychomotor retardation of prolonged duration. If these are present, a referral to a bereavement counselor or grief therapist is needed.

Most often, these professionals can be identified through a local hospital, hospice organization, or mental health agency. Many professional organizations with state or national offices, such as the Association for Death Education and Counseling (ADEC) or the National Association of Social Workers (NASW), can also be a source of information about how to obtain professional help. Once potential sources have been identified, it may take repeated efforts to actually link the distressed individual or family to the appropriate source. For some individuals, it may suffice simply to pass the information along, but it is usually more helpful to provide them with specific information or a specific name, with details on why or how that resource can help. This type of information, along with words of encouragement to use available resources, will help ensure that the referral is successful.

What interventions and programs are helpful in dealing with normal and complicated grief?

A variety of programs, interventions, and resources to address the distinctive needs of grieving individuals have been developed over the past three decades.

The continuum of bereavement interventions includes:

- Preventive interventions (anticipatory grieving, education, emotional support)
- Monitoring with social support
- Support groups (including online and telephone groups)
- Brief supportive or bereavement counseling
- Grief therapy or psychotherapy (individual, couples, or family therapy)

These interventions can be viewed as addressing needs along a continuum from normal bereavement to complicated bereavement. It is important, when considering interventions to assist the bereaved, to match the level and type of service to need. This ensures that those whose bereavement is more complicated receive the care that will best address their needs (Walsh-Burke, 2000).

Preventive interventions

Sometimes individuals or families facing a loss experience anticipatory reactions of anxiety or sadness as well as social isolation. This is particularly true in situations where a life-limiting illness or condition is prolonged or painful. Provision of information about normal grief reactions as well as practical and emotional support can reduce feelings of isolation or disenfranchisement and may help those who do not have a framework for understanding their own, or their loved ones', reactions.

Monitoring, with social support

In some hospitals and most hospices, routine telephone contacts with surviving family members are made within a specified time period to check in and assess their adjustment. Hospice bereavement protocol calls for these contacts for one year following the death. The contacts are usually very welcomed by those who are grieving, as they provide social support from someone who understands the grieving process and provide the opportunity to monitor whether "bereavement is proceeding normally or if complications have arisen" (Blum, 1993, p. 121–122). Engagement of the bereaved family member in further counseling or a referral for grief therapy can then be provided if needed.

Bereavement support groups

Bereavement support groups are offered by many organizations both locally and nationally. These groups have the same goals as support groups aimed at other life situations. Support group goals include reducing isolation, relieving psychosocial distress, and enhancing coping skills. In many agencies these groups are facilitated by professional social workers or psychologists, but some are led by trained volunteers who themselves have experienced grief. The techniques used by group facilitators include providing information and education about normal and complicated grief, encouraging mutual support and sharing of feelings, and reinforcing the use of effective coping strategies.

Most local communities have hospices that offer bereavement groups not only to families they have served but to other members of the community as well. Hospice bereavement counselors can also be helpful in finding additional resources, such as grief therapists, in your community. Many hospitals and palliative care programs also offer bereavement support groups. Some communities have Grief Centers and many of these offer groups to their own local community members as well as to those who live at a distance. Some bereavement groups are listed in the Internet Resources for this chapter. Telephone support groups or online support groups offered by these organizations can be particularly helpful to those in small communities where a teen bereavement support group, for example, might not be available.

Not all bereavement support groups follow the same model, but a fairly standard group might span six to eight sessions that include the following topics:

Session I: Getting acquainted, reviewing the group purpose and guidelines
Session II: Sharing loss experiences
Session III: An overview of normal grief in children, adolescents and adults
Session IV: Coping with anxiety and depression
Session V: Stress management
Session VI: Finding hope
Session VII: Ending, saying goodbye

Support groups are also helpful for people grieving losses that are not related to death. Many organizations offer support groups for adults who are divorcing and schools sometimes offer groups for children and teens whose families are going through divorce or relocation. These groups may have a similar time frame and structure as bereavement support groups and share the purpose of helping to support group members in adjusting to the changes associated with these life transitions.

Individual or family bereavement counseling

Bereavement counseling is provided to assist a mourner in completing the tasks of grieving. This kind of help can be provided by a variety of trained counselors, including peer counselors, pastoral care providers, psychologists, and social workers. While most people are able to complete the tasks of grieving without bereavement counseling, at times the nature of the loss or the social situation of the affected individual can make it difficult. Bereavement counseling often consists of:

- Encouraging the bereaved to tell their story and share memories
- Acknowledging and giving permission to express feelings
- Identifying strategies to cope with the effects of grief, such as relaxation training
- Helping the bereaved person to plan for their life without the deceased.

The bereavement counselor can help the survivor in a variety of ways. Telling the story can help the survivor come to grips with the loss, since sharing the details can make the loss experience more "real." The counselor's support during the telling of the story and the expression of feelings can help to reinforce the mourner's coping efforts through identification of previously effective strategies and teaching of new strategies. During counseling, the survivor is also helped to identify and express feelings such as anger and helplessness that are difficult for many people to express. Many survivors also express feelings of guilt and the counselor can help with reality testing when the survivor may have difficulty seeing the situation rationally. Feelings of sadness and anxiety are often expressed by survivors during counseling.

Perhaps the best endorsement for the healing power of expressing emotions related to grief comes from Morrie Schwartz, the retired Brandeis University professor immortalized in Mitch Albom's best-selling book *Tuesdays with Morrie*.

Morrie, who is facing death from a debilitating illness, encourages individuals facing loss not to hold back their emotions.

If you hold back on emotions—if you don't allow yourself to go all the way through them—you can never get to being detached, you're too busy being afraid. You're afraid of the pain, you're afraid of the grief. . . . But, by throwing yourself into these emotions, by allowing yourself to dive in all the way, over your head even, you experience them fully and completely. You know what pain is. You know what love is. You know what grief is. And only then can you say, 'All right. I have experienced that emotion. I recognize that emotion. Now I need to detach from that emotion for a moment' (Albom, 1997, p. 104).

Another technique used by bereavement counselors, in addition to verbal counseling, is writing letters of farewell to the deceased. This can be especially helpful when the grieving individual did not have an opportunity to say goodbye in person. Poetry and journal writing are also useful techniques, along with drawing, role-playing and relaxation training.

In addition to providing support and utilizing these techniques for facilitating completion of the tasks of grieving, the bereavement counselor can help to interpret the experiences of the bereaved person, provide reassurance about the normalcy of the grief process, and assess the coping and adjustment of the bereaved. If the bereaved person is unable to cope effectively with the support of bereavement counseling or manifests complicated grief, the bereavement counselor may make a referral for grief therapy.

Grief therapy

Complicated grief may require grief therapy, which is more intensive than bereavement counseling. Many grief therapists use psychodynamic therapy models to help clients gain insight into the source of their distress regarding attachment and loss. Interpersonal therapy and Bowenian family therapy are also models used in helping individuals and families deal with complicated bereavement, which often involves unresolved past losses.

Frank et al. (1997) developed a specific intervention program to treat bereaved individuals who meet the criteria for a major depressive episode. The nine-session intervention is based on treatment for Post-traumatic stress disorder and includes reliving the moment of the death, saying goodbye to the deceased, and exposure to situations the bereaved person had been avoiding since the death (such as the cemetery).

Noting the family's primary role in caring for the terminally ill, Kissane et al. (1998) developed their model of family grief therapy. At-risk families are identified through screening, and a focused, time-limited intervention runs for six to eight sessions (1.5 hours each) over the course of about six months. The goals are to increase cohesion, conflict resolution, and the expression of thoughts and feelings. According to the authors, this therapy progresses through five phases: (1) assessment (2) identification of relevant issues emerging from the initial phase of grief (3) focused treatment (4) consolidation of coping skills, and (5) ending. Most of the therapists who perform this type of therapy are social workers carefully trained in the model. Children experiencing complicated grief can benefit from play therapy that includes equipment such as sand trays and puppets (Gil, 1998; Webb, 1996).

Psychiatric referrals and use of psychotropic medication

Sometimes grief therapy alone is not sufficient and is supplemented with psychiatric treatment, particularly with persons suffering from a major depression or other psychiatric disorder. Researchers have demonstrated that the combined use of psychotherapy plus an antidepressant medication produces the best relief from severe depression (Reynolds, 1999).

Some psychiatrists provide both therapy and medication, while others work in collaboration with a primary grief therapist to provide consultation on medication and medical conditions that may be influencing the distressed individual. If someone you know is experiencing significant depression, anxiety, or other symptoms of serious distress, a referral to either an experienced grief therapist who works closely with a psychiatrist or to a psychiatrist who specializes in grief therapy is important.

Innovative interventions

Some organizations present daylong workshops as a valuable addition to current counseling alternatives for the bereaved (Beem, 1998). Annual memorial services held at hospitals or hospices have been well received by bereaved persons as a formal ritual where they can remember their lost loved one and be reunited with staff who cared for the patient. These services often include a candle lighting ceremony or memorial ritual, such as writing the names of those who have died on a star or quilt square that are then displayed together with an array of other names and images. This type of visual reminder provides a sense of shared experience and helps to reinforce the support and understanding that community members can offer one another.

Retreat programs and even camp programs have been utilized to assist individuals and families through the grieving process (Morrison, 1999). Creative means of expressing grief are often included in these programs. Writing down thoughts and feelings in a journal is helpful for many people. Some bereavement programs encourage those who have lost someone to write a letter to the person who has died, expressing the feelings they may not have had a chance to express before the death. This type of activity, when guided by an experienced bereavement counselor, can bring a sense of relief as well as a sense of shared support when written and read in a group. Children, as well as adolescents and adults, may also experience relief from the opportunity to express themselves through art, using materials such as watercolor or acrylic paint, markers, stamp kits, or clay. Sometimes the art that is produced becomes a keepsake or special reminder of the person who is no longer present, or it can serve as a gift to others who are grieving the loss of that person. Sometimes it is simply the experience of expressing feelings through drawing or painting that brings relief and the piece that is produced is not as important as the process of creating the work. Suggested expressive activities are included in Appendix F.

For those who may have difficulty expressing their feelings, it can be helpful to read the thoughts or feelings of others who have written about their experiences of loss. Bowman (1999) compiled a list of literary resources for bereavement. He presented the rationale that grief counseling frequently involves the "storying" and "restorying" of lives; hence, "the stories of others, even those found in literature, can provoke feelings or thoughts about one's own story" (p. 51). Using various subtopics such as "Healing, Hope, and Acceptance," Bowman presents poems, quotes, and literary sources that may be useful in reflecting on, and accepting, difficult feelings. A list of books and videos that can be used by individuals or groups are included in Appendix B of this text.

Two of my social work colleagues at Cancer Care in New York developed an innovative way to use music in counseling teenagers coping with the loss of a family member. They suggest that teens bring to their sessions a piece of music that evokes strong feelings for them. The teenagers listen to the music together and then talk about how and why the music evokes these feelings and what other songs might be helpful (Levine, 1999).

With the advent and rapid growth of the Internet, support groups are now sometimes conducted online. Organizations such as Cancer Care and Griefnet offer online groups that are facilitated by professionals or trained peer leaders. These offerings include bereavement groups for adults and teens. Many people also now participate in online chat rooms that focus on grief and loss. Few of these chat rooms, however, are monitored or facilitated by trained professionals. Because it is impossible to assess the quality of leadership or emotional stability of the participants in these forums, it is important to encourage anyone using the Internet for information or support to investigate the credibility of the source being used and to exercise caution and self-protection when using these resources.

Exercise: Identifying Signs of Normal and Complicated Grief

The four tasks of grieving identified by Worden were discussed in this chapter. They are 1) acceptance of the loss; 2) experiencing the pain of grief; 3) adjusting to the new environment without the person who was lost; 4) relocating and memorializing the loved one.

Part 1: Normal Grief

Think of someone you know who has experienced a death. Using the normal emotions of grief as a checklist, note whether the person showed signs of sadness, anger, or guilt that are a part of normal grief. Describe your observations, either in a group discussion or in writing.

Part 2: Complicated Grief

Worden notes that complicated grief results when those who experience a loss do not complete the four tasks of grieving. Choose a movie to watch from the list below. (Each depicts individuals who are grieving a loss, actual or symbolic.) As you view the movie note the signs of complicated grief that you observe. (For example, in the film *Antwone Fisher*, Antwone is referred to a psychiatrist when he evidences unresolved grief through his angry, aggressive behavior following multiple losses in his childhood.)

Corinna, Corinna (Young girl grieving the death of a parent)

Fearless (Parent grieving the death of a child)

Ponette (Young girl grieving the death of a parent)

Smoke Signals (Adult son grieving the loss of his father)

Life as a House (Adolescent son grieving first the divorce of his parents and then his father's death)

Garden State (Adolescent son grieving the death of his mother following a disabling accident)

Antwone Fisher (Young adult grieving multiple childhood losses, including loss of biological family due to foster care placement)

Ordinary People (Adolescent son grieving the death of his sibling)

Part 3: Discussion

Discuss in small groups, or describe in writing, the signs of complicated grief you have observed in the first two parts of this exercise. Describe the type of complicated grief the individuals may be evidencing, and the interventions that might be helpful to them to complete the tasks of grieving

Self-Test

1. Which of the following is NOT a risk factor for complicated grief?
   a. Family conflict before a death
   b. Disenfranchised loss
   c. Cultural differences
   d. Multiple stressors at the time of loss

1. According to the Diagnostic and Statistical Manual of Mental Disorders, bereavement may be complicated by major depression when which of the following is present?
   a. Diminished interest in daily activities
   b. Morbid preoccupation with worthlessness
   c. Weight loss
   d. Diminished ability to concentrate

Answers 1) c 2) b

Internet Resources

The National Cancer Institute provides an overview of grief, loss, and bereavement, as well as information about complicated bereavement and grief at different stages of development, and other topics in the Physician's Query section of their Web site. http://www.cancer.gov/cancerinfo/pdq/supportivecare/bereavement/HealthProfessional

Cancer Care, along with other organizations, provides telephone and online support groups for those who are grieving. For information visit http://www.cancercare.org

Concerns of Police Survivors is one example of an organization that provides peer support and grief retreats to assist families of officers slain in the line of duty at http://www.nationalcops.org/

The Association for Death Education and Counseling offers information and training related to bereavement. Training workshops can be found at http://www.adec.org

The National Association of Social Workers can assist in locating trained clinical social workers who provide counseling through their Register of Clinical Social Workers at http://www.naswdc.org

References _____

Albom, M. (1997). *Tuesdays with Morrie*. New York: Doubleday.

American Psychiatric Association. (2000). *Diagnostic and statistical manual of mental disorders-TR* (4th ed.). Washington, DC: American Psychiatric Association.

Beem, E., Eurelings-Bontekoe, E., Cleiren, M., & Garssen, B. (1998). Workshops to support the bereavement process. *Patient education & counseling, 34*(1), 53–62.

Blum, D. (1993). Social work services for adult cancer patients and their families. In M. Lauria, P. Fogelberg, J. Herman, & N. Stearns (Eds.), *Oncology social work: A clinician's guide* (pp. 101–134). Atlanta, GA: American Cancer Society, Inc.

Bowlby, J. (1973). *Attachment and loss: Separation, anxiety and anger* (vol. 2). New York: Basic Books.

Bowman, T. (1999). Literary resources for bereavement. *Hospice Journal, 14*(1), 39–54.

Cambell, S. (2002). Does therapy prolong the agony? *Psychology Today, 35*(4), 28.

Frank, E., Prigerson, H., Shear, M., & Reynolds III, C. (1997). Phenomenology and treatment of bereavement-related distress in the elderly. *Int clin psychopharmacol, 12*(7), 25–9.

Freud, S. (1917). Mourning and melancholia. In *The Pelican Freud Library*, 11 (1984). *On metapsychology: The theory of psychoanalysis* (pp. 245–68). London: Penguin.

Gil, E. (1998). *Working through trauma with play*. New York: Guilford Press.

Kelly, B., Edwards, P., Synott, R., Neil, C., Baillie, R., & Battistutta, D. (1999). Predictors of bereavement outcome for family careers of cancer patients. *Psychooncology, 8*(3), 237–249.

Kirby, M. (1999). Grief in the law enforcement workplace: The police experience. In K. Davidson & K. Doka (Eds.), *Living with grief: At work, at school, at worship* (pp. 29–44). Washington, DC: The Hospice Foundation of America.

Kissane, D., Bloch, S., McKenzie, M., McDowall, A. C., & Nitzan, R. (1998). Family grief therapy: A preliminary account of a new model to promote healthy family functioning during palliative care and bereavement. *Psychooncology, 7*(1), 14–25.

Kubler-Ross, E. (1997). *On death and dying* (reprint ed.). New York: Scribner.

Levine, A., Sutton, A., Keller, J. & Nessim, S. (1999). *It's a quarter to three, no one in the session 'cept the teen and me: Music that soothes the adolescent beast*. New Orleans, LA: Association of Oncology Social Work Annual Conference.

Lindemann, E. (1944). Symptomatology and management of acute grief. *American Journal of Psychiatry, 101*, 141–148.

Moos, R., & Moos, B. (1981). *Family environment scale manual*. Palo Alto: Consulting Psychologists Press.

Morrison, M. J. (1999). Camp good grief. *Bereavement: A magazine of hope and healing* (May–June). Retrieved January 20, 2004 from http://www.bereavementmag.com/magazine/archives/viewarticle.asp?ArticleID=640

Pelzar, D. (1997). *The lost boy*. Deerfield Beach, FL: Health Communications, Inc.

Rando, T. (1984). *Grief, dying, and death: Clinical interventions for caregivers*. Champaign, IL: Research Press Company.

Rando, T. (1993). *Treatment of complicated mourning*. Champaign, IL: Research Press.

Reynolds III, C., Miller, M., Pasternak, R., Frank, E., Perel, J., Cornes, C., Houck, P., Mazumdar, S., Dew, M., & Kupfer, D. (1999). Treatment of bereavement-related major depressive episodes in later life: A controlled study of acute and continuation treatment with nortriptyline and interpersonal psychotherapy. *American Journal of Psychiatry, 156*(2), 202–208.

Schraffenberger, B. (2000). *Spotlight*. Comfort Candles Newsletter. Cincinnati, OH: Comfort Candles Corp.

Walsh-Burke, K. (2000). Matching bereavement services to level of need. *The Hospice Journal, 15*(1), 77–86.

Webb, N. B. (Ed.). (1999). *Play therapy with children in crisis, second edition: Individual, group, and family treatment*. New York: Guilford Press.

Worden, W. (2002). *Grief counseling and grief therapy: A handbook for the mental health practitioner*. (3rd ed). New York: Springer Publishing Company.

5

Cultural and Spiritual Influences

We must accept finite disappointment, but never lose infinite hope.

—Martin Luther King, Jr.

The Influence of Culture in Coping with Loss and Grief

As part of the self-assessment exercise in Chapter 2, you were asked to think back to your experiences related to loss. There is a good chance that in doing this, you described ways of coping with loss that were significantly influenced by your cultural and spiritual background. When I have assigned this exercise to students in my classes, the memories that frequently stand out are those of religious or spiritual practices, such as a wake or memorial service that they attended as young children, and many of these spiritual practices are recollected in the context of culture.

For example, in a class discussion a student reflected on her experiences:

I am part Native American (Cherokee) and African. I have roots in South Carolina. Our traditions and food are southern in distinction. Typically each person visiting a family who has recently suffered a loss would bring a dish of their best effort. Religion in the south is just as fun and light as any social event up north would be. It is an inherently natural way of holding the family together. It fosters common and traditional values and mores for the community and the family. My upbringing included religion, and holidays were for bringing out the tablecloth and my mother's best effort at southern cooking. My mother can cook and make cakes from scratch like you would not believe. Our tradition

includes the return to the church for spiritual guidance and fellowsi..
black funeral with song and reading, with a gathering at the home afterwar..
wakes were sad during the service but after the service ended it was clear that u.
socialization at the home of the deceased was for a more lively presentation. It .
uncommon for the family to have libation and laughter, just like a party at some home..
My family usually just has good food and good stories (Butler-Jones, 2003).

Culture and spirituality are discussed together in this chapter because they are often intertwined and sometimes inseparable. Even though your own cultural and spiritual experiences may be distinct, as they may be for many of the people you find yourself assisting, it is important to understand how both culture and spirituality can influence reactions to loss.

Culture is a complex concept. For this discussion, the description used by the National Association of Social Workers is helpful. "The word culture. . .implies *the integrated pattern of human behavior that includes thoughts, communications, actions, customs, beliefs, values, and institutions of a racial, ethnic, religious, or social group. Culture is often referred to as the totality of ways that are passed down from one generation to another*" (NASW, 2005). In addition, it is helpful to know that some people define their cultural group through identification communities, the members of which share common experiences. Examples are individuals who identify with deaf culture, or individuals who identify themselves with gay culture, in addition to cultural groups based on ethnicity such as Mexican-American. Awareness of the cultural group with which an individual or family identifies is very important for professionals who want to assist with grief because the beliefs, values, and behavioral norms to which they have been socialized will most likely influence their responses to loss. Culture may also influence how an individual or family regards professionals and their offers of help. For example, a French-Canadian member of our interdisciplinary hospice team acknowledged that in her family of origin self-sufficiency is highly valued and accepting help from those outside the immediate family is sometimes difficult because it is viewed as contradictory to this value. Her perspective was helpful to other members of the team in better understanding the meaning of accepting a hospice referral to a family in our community who shared her French-Canadian background.

Most professional training programs now emphasize cultural competence, or at least cultural sensitivity, in preparing professionals for practice in a multicultural society. In your professional training you have most likely already begun to study and practice within this framework. For the purposes of this discussion of grief, **cultural sensitivity** is a term used to describe *an awareness of, and appreciation for, the differences in values, beliefs, and norms of people from different cultural and spiritual backgrounds.* **Cultural competence** implies that professionals practice cultural sensitivity, but are also able *to engage and interact effectively with people from diverse cultural backgrounds.* Awareness of cultural norms can aid in providing assistance that demonstrates respect and understanding. Failure to understand and acknowledge cultural differences can be perceived as disrespect and may impede a therapist's ability to be helpful.

A school counselor writes about some of the cultural differences she has encountered:

Chapter 5

I came to the United States from Portugal when I was an elementary school student. When I first attended a funeral in the U.S. that was not for a Portuguese person, I couldn't believe the differences from my own culture, from beginning to end. For example, something as simple as attire can be viewed in extremely different ways. In my culture one always wears black out of respect for the mourners regardless of whether you are family or not. When my neighbor's son died, she wore colorful clothing to the funeral and I was shocked. Coming from my frame of reference, that symbolized disrespect and lack of feeling. At home, after the funeral, she changed into a housedress that was multicolored with very vibrant colors. I know that the color you wear outside has nothing to do with feelings of loss (or the color one may feel on the inside) yet it was culturally shocking to me.

I have also found the funerals for Americans that I have attended to be more reserved. In Portugal, in my experience, one witnesses the arrival of the casket into the church being carried by close friends or family, and you then escort the casket to the burial ground (cemetery) and witness its descent into the ground while mourners sob and scream. Here in the U.S. (at least at the funerals I have attended), the family is more likely to grieve and mourn in private; there is less public display. It is important to be aware that everyone handles death in a very different way and one cannot judge how someone else feels or infer how someone feels by looking at them or their behavior from the outside (Silva, 2002).

As this observation indicates, a lack of awareness of different cultural groups' responses to loss can lead us to:

- Misinterpret an individual's or family's reactions.
- Fail to offer support or assistance that might be perceived as helpful.
- Offend the grieving person(s) and create a barrier to their receiving care and support.

There is perhaps no better illustration of this kind of error than the situation described in Anne Fadiman's (1998) book *The Spirit Catches You and You Fall Down.* Fadiman recounts how the many professionals involved in caring for a three year-old Hmong child with epilepsy did so without understanding her family's cultural beliefs and practices. Everyone suffered as a result. The parents were deprived of the understanding and support they sought, and the medical providers felt frustrated at their inability to intervene and prolong the child's life. Yet, it is reasonable to question how any individual or team can possibly expect to become knowledgeable about the literally hundreds of cultural groups whose members you may encounter in your work (Irish, 1993).

It is also important to recognize that knowledge of a particular *group* does not necessarily equip someone to adequately understand an *individual,* who may not subscribe to the beliefs or norms of the group. Even someone from a similar cultural background cannot assume that their own perspective applies to someone else. Some members of the same cultural group, for example, have different spiritual practices or subscribe to different norms based on factors such as socioeconomic status or multiple group memberships, or individual ideology.

Therefore, most experts in cross-cultural practice suggest that the best approach to working with individuals from diverse backgrounds is to ask them what values, beliefs, and practices are important to them. Expression of sorrow for a person's loss is almost always appropriate, followed by a general statement such as, "I would like to help in any way that I can. Perhaps you can tell me what you or your family would prefer." If you are planning to attend a memorial or visit with a grieving person, it is usually helpful to find out how best to show respect or what kind of behavior is expected in mourners in their culture, but be aware that there may be other expectations that you can't anticipate. To learn as much as you can, Koenig and Gates-Williams (1995) recommend making use of available resources, including community or religious leaders, family members, and language translators. Another member of your staff who is familiar with cultural norms may also be able to give you information.

As a beginning social worker, I was fortunate to have spent the first two years of my career working in a Jewish rehabilitation hospital, even though I was raised in the Roman Catholic faith. Shabbat services were held every Friday at sundown and a kosher menu was provided for residents and their visiting family members. My first supervisor, along with the hospital's rabbi and the families I worked with, were instrumental in helping me learn about Shivva and the mourning rituals that take place for seven days following a death. During this time, family members mourn at home and visitors bring food and comfort to them. Orthodox families covered the mirrors in the home, wore black clothing, and observed other practices that were very different from those I had observed in my own childhood. Acknowledging my lack of information enabled me to learn about this and the many other rituals related to death so that I could show respect and assist grieving residents and families, despite our differences.

Over the years I have learned a great deal from colleagues with diverse backgrounds who have shared their experiences related to grief and mourning. For example, one colleague shared that when her grandfather died in their family's small village in the Philippines, the whole community came together, rubbed his body with oils, dressed his body in linens, made a crown of flowers, and paraded around the small community. Following this there was a celebration with food, singing, storytelling, dancing, and prayer.

Another colleague writes:

> My experience with death has been affected by cultural attitudes. In my Latino culture the response to death is an intense one. When a person has died in the Puerto Rican culture we can expect overwhelming responses by family and the Hispanic community. The visual I have of Puerto Rican funerals is of women standing around the deceased in an emotional uproar and of ambulances on standby outside the funeral parlor. My eight-year-old daughter was so affected by the emotional responses of the Latina women in our family when her father's brother died that we made the choice not to have her participate in any of the funerary rituals. My experience also has been that the more tragic the death the more intense the response will be by family and loved ones. Intense grief reactions by individuals around me make the experience of death for me unpleasant (Elias, 2003).

A student in a class discussion shared a very different perspective after attending a funeral in which intense emotion was expressed following a tragic death.

Every aspect of this funeral was unlike any other that I have attended. There were over 1500 people in attendance. Prior to the service the family had been there to view the body and there was time after that for others to view. As the service started the family of about 150 extended members paraded down the aisle to reserved seats in the front. There was a very large choir that sang, several friends gave speeches, and there was a lot of dancing involved. I do not remember what religion the family was, but the focus of the service was on eternal life and the preacher focused on celebration rather than mourning. There were nurses present because people got so in touch with the "holy spirit" that they would pass out. I have never been to such a ceremony before. It was unreal, the spirit in the room, over someone that had died. The service lasted about four hours and following was a reception with all kinds of food sponsored by my agency. It was a beautiful commemoration (Baron, 2003).

A colleague who attended the funeral of a Mashantucket Pequot tribal elder shared her observations. The elder was buried in her full Native American tribal dress. There were pastors from various churches who each spoke about her life and the things she had done to help others. The funeral was a celebration of her life and called a "homegoing"—or a celebration of her transition from the natural life on earth to a spiritual life in heaven with God. The funeral had lively music with singing and dancing.

Yet another student informed me about Buddhist practices. She explained that in the Buddhist tradition death is seen as an inevitable part of a larger process of nature's cycles, of which human manifestation is but a small part. Prayer is not offered to a being outside oneself, but the ritual of chanting is used as a tool for cleansing one's consciousness. Beliefs in life after death include the teaching that one's thoughts, words, and actions leave an imprint on one's consciousness, and that rebirth (life after death) is a manifestation of the energies related to those imprints. Buddhists believe that the spirit hovers over the body for three days after death, so the body is not moved for three days. It is also believed that touching the body (except for cleansing) could disturb the spirit. Chanting is believed to liberate the spirit and may continue for long periods.

Learning about these different practices, and learning more about what is unfamiliar to me, has been essential in my own professional development. The Internet also now offers many excellent sources of information. Many diverse cultural groups and professional organizations provide information and guidance on their Web sites. Some of these are listed in the Internet resources at the end of this chapter. Professional organizations are also developing standards for culturally competent practice or cross-cultural practice to guide their members. The National Association of Social Workers, for example, has published Standards for Cultural Competence on their Web site. Many medical organizations publish both standards of practice and information about different cultural practices related to grief, since health care professionals interact frequently with diverse populations and grief is commonly experienced in health care settings. A universal set of standards has been developed by the U.S. government's Office of Minority Health to guide all health professionals in cultural competence. Web sites like EthnoMed.org provide specific information about different cultural groups that include mourning practices.

Before more specifically addressing spirituality, it is important to discuss one more aspect of culture and its influence on grieving individuals. A male colleague alluded to the influence of our contemporary American culture in the perspective he offered on gender and grief. He noted that for men in America it is often difficult to grieve a loss in the same way that women do, because many men are taught from an early age not to show emotions such as sadness, loneliness, or depression. He noted that many men he has worked with, when faced with the overwhelming feelings of loss of a loved one, are unable to cope with the feelings they are experiencing and may not have healthy outlets to express their emotions. This perspective also reminds us that cultural messages are transmitted in many ways, not only through direct family communication or interaction. Many grief experts note that the mass media in the United States has a tremendous influence on our ideas about how to react in the face of loss. The way the media commonly focuses on violent death in the news, movies, and television programs, and generally omits any mention of the long-term effects on survivors or healthy longer-term mourning practices, is believed by some to contribute to a "grief denying" culture.

Many students, when reflecting on the influence of the media on their own perceptions of death and loss, acknowledge that they may have learned to avoid the topic of grief, partly as a result of their exposure to mass media. Cartoons, for example, often show characters undergoing traumatic injuries only to reappear, unscathed, in the next scene or episode. Similarly, in television programs and computer games, people are annihilated with no reference to the grief experienced by survivors. There are some movies that have depicted both realistic and positive models of grieving individuals and families with diverse backgrounds. A few of these, such as *Smoke Signals,* are included as suggestions in this chapter's exercise.

One other very important point that has been underscored by many of my students and colleagues is that many children in the U.S. as well as in other countries grow up in a culture of violence, in which actual death and loss are a constant part of daily life. One student articulately expressed her concern that our current grief theories and textbooks, and many professionals working with children and families, do not effectively address this issue. In a class discussion, a student assertively voiced her thoughts and feelings about this topic and gave all of us in the class much food for thought. She said that there was a gap for her in the theories of grief we had been studying and that there is NOTHING she would like and appreciate more than for grief experts to explain to her the culture of poverty as it relates to the ghetto and the pain of waking up and living another day, facing an endless accumulation of losses. She asked the instructor and the class if we could help her to understand how and why there is so much news coverage about violence in a foreign country, but so little coverage about the culture of violence in our own country, cities, neighborhoods, communities, and homes. She added that it frightens her that people can ignore such pain, loss, and suffering. Who are we fooling? The pain and suffering exist but they are only addressed when they spread to more affluent communities (e.g., school shootings). She asked those of us in the class not to take her views personally, but suggested that we all need to start understanding what it is like to feel worthless, hopeless, and extremely angry about poverty and violence in our society. This student, and many others who live and work in communities where poverty, violence, and multiple losses are prevalent, have made me increasingly aware of how little attention is given to the grief of vulnerable populations.

This is an area where much more work is needed, including needs assessments, research, and program development. For those of us working with children and families exposed to daily and often traumatic losses, we can begin by acknowledging these losses. We must also raise our voices to advocate for, and participate in, community action and change to prevent this injustice from continuing in our society.

The Influence of Spirituality in Coping with Loss and Grief

In an interview about integrating spirituality into medical interviews, Christina Puchalsky, a physician who has developed a spiritual assessment tool, explains why spirituality became important to her, as a member of the helping professions:

> Well, I think I have been very fortunate to have very spiritual parents, who themselves are from Europe and experienced World War II in powerful ways, including a lot of losses. I grew up with people who have used their own spiritual beliefs to help them cope with difficult things and to find meaning in life. Although they have a religion—they are Catholic—it wasn't really the focus on the religion ever, it was a focus on a much broader concept. I was never raised with [the notion] 'There's only one God and the Catholic one is the right one.' Never. My parents have given me great role modeling on the role of spirituality and have allowed me to search extensively. I was going to convert to Judaism, so I explored that for a while. My dad and I went to Hindu temples together; we explored that faith. You know, I learned Eastern meditation by myself and with him, so I've done lots of different things. I was involved in a Tibetan Buddhist monastery throughout my 20s, so I've explored many different religious and spiritual beliefs and practices, and have throughout the course of my life been with people of many different beliefs. Some are religious, some are not, and I've just always been very interested in spirituality. So based on those experiences, as well as several major deaths of significant people in my life—all of these experiences are part of the background of my interest in integrating a spiritual history into the medical interview (Romer, 1999).

An American student's observations about the way people in Ecuador acknowledge death serves as an example of how culture and spirituality are both important in grief reactions and are often intertwined. In a class discussion, the student shared that she had spent two months in Ecuador and attended a university course for Americans about Ecuadorian culture. She learned that families in Ecuador celebrate death by having a picnic on the grave of the deceased loved one, making a plate for the deceased individual and leaving it as an offering. It was explained to the American students that through this ritual, the family members are celebrating life and feeding the soul of their loved one who has gone on to the next life. Every year, Ecuadorians celebrate The Day of the Dead where they have another picnic on the grave of their loved ones and continue the feeding of the soul. She remarked that it is interesting how Americans think of death in very negative aspects, while Ecuadorian culture celebrates death.

It is now recognized that spirituality and religion are very important influences in peoples' lives, particularly in coping with death and loss. Rabbi Earl Grollman (1996) has written, "When unexpected crises shatter lives, people of all faiths often ask the same questions: 'Is it God's will? If God's will is for life, why did this terrible death occur?' (p. 2)." Yet, professionals and laypersons alike have difficulty defining the concepts of both spirituality and religion. Until recently, the two terms were sometimes used interchangeably and few professional training programs emphasized religion or spirituality. In the last two decades, however, both popular media and professional literature have paid a great deal more attention to the distinction between religion and the broader concept of spirituality.

While the term **spirituality** has been used in different ways, many training programs now use a broad, inclusive definition of *that which gives meaning to one's life and draws one to transcend oneself.* **Religion**, on the other hand, is defined more narrowly as a *communal or institutional expression or practice of faith.*

Highfield, Mudd, and Millson (1992) suggest that spirituality is a broader concept than religion, and that religion is one expression of spirituality. Other expressions of spirituality include prayer, meditation, interactions with others or nature, and a relationship with God or a higher power. Spirituality is considered by many to be important in helping both those who are dying and those who are grieving a loss to make meaning of life.

The Gallup Poll has been asking the American public about the role of religion in their lives since 1952. In more recent polls questions about spirituality have also been asked. In a 2001 poll, 55% of those sampled reported religion to be very important in their lives, while 30% reported fairly important, and 15% reported not very important. When asked what best described their beliefs: religious, spiritual but not religious, neither, both religious and spiritual, or no opinion, 54% of those sampled selected religious, 30% selected spiritual but not religious, only 9% selected neither, and 6% answered both. Only 1% responded no opinion. In addition, when asked if religion is outdated or whether it can answer all or most of today's problems, 63% of the respondents answered yes (Gallup Poll, 2000, retrieved May 5, 2000 from http://www.gallup.com/poll/indicators/indreligion.asp).

It is therefore crucial to take into consideration, and be informed about, religion and spirituality when assisting individuals, families, and communities in coping with grief and loss. A Vietnamese student writes:

> I remember the first time that I experienced death more than ten years ago when I was a young teenager and one of my best friends died in an accident. I still remember the feeling of pain that I felt inside of me when I attended her funeral. I cried for many days after her death, and I asked myself what she did to deserve death? Because we were prohibited in my family from discussing the topics of death or dying, I didn't get any advice on what to do to cope with her death. After her death, I felt more appreciative of what I had in life right then, and I still do at this moment. I believe in reincarnation, and I hope that I can be reunited with my best friend in our next lives (Tran, 2003).

An African American from the southern region of the United States writes:

> In our southern African American culture, a funeral service is held and is called a 'home going.' The church affiliates, the pastor, and friends provide support in many ways. They bring food, listen, and talk—whatever is needed. The ceremony is religious in nature. Within this tradition, Christians live on in spirit and it is believed that their souls go on to be with the Almighty, according to the King James Version of the Bible. The activity that takes place before the actual burial is called a processional. All immediate family members walk into the church to view the body in an open casket (this is optional, but typical). The family members walk through the church, almost as in a parade, and their grief is displayed publicly. At this service people are asked to share a few words about the deceased, and a song, usually a solo, is sung. Then the minister or pastor speaks to the family about the deceased and offers condolences. The body is then taken to the burial place and a parade of cars, with their lights on, follows closely behind. The body is placed in the ground and flowers laid over it (DeVeux, 2002).

Another student shared her experiences with a range of different spiritually based funerary ceremonies:

> I have attended a range of services/ceremonies marking the rite of passage from death to life. Services have been held in the Native American, Jewish, Catholic, and Protestant traditions. The one I found most powerful and healing occurred eight months ago when a fellow supervisor died in a car crash. His family conducted a private ceremony in Utah, and my agency conducted a Native American memorial service based on his form of spirituality. It began with a native mourning song, which, though sung in native language, invoked strong feelings of sadness, putting mourners in touch with their feelings. Following the song, a Native American prayer was read which symbolized the spiritual journey, the return to Mother Earth, and the concept of acceptance. Another coworker played a native song on his guitar, which stirred feelings of comfort and connectedness. Mourners consisting of colleagues, friends, and clients were given an opportunity to speak in his remembrance. Most powerful were the words of his clients whose lives he had so deeply touched. A final ritual was offered which involved dropping a stone into a large, round clay pot full of water, and through the rippling effect meditating on how we had each been affected by his presence, as well as our overall interconnectedness with each other (Davis, 2003).

While families within many cultural groups and spiritual communities embrace the same mourning rituals, it is not uncommon for members of a family to practice religion or express their spirituality differently. Factors other than culture and spirituality also influence individuals to respond differently than those around them. These differences can be disconcerting and even cause conflict within a grieving family. Therefore each individual may need validation for their own way of dealing with loss.

> In the African American church culture that I grew up in, we celebrate the life of the person through the ritual of a funeral. In the black church, specifically the Pentecostal movement, if one dies in the faith, meaning they have accepted that Jesus Christ was born, lived, and died for the sins of the world, they have lived a life believing and hear-

ing that death is a part of living but death is not final. Death is viewed as "sleepin'" and the service is called a "home going," for it is a celebration of the life of the deceased. Services are a wonderful way of bringing closure to death, or at least acting as a beginning of closure. When my grandmother died, her last wishes were that she be cremated. She was a Jehovah's Witness and we did not worship or celebrate death the same way. At her service, we were made to feel by members of the Jehovah's Witness community that we shouldn't grieve. My family was told that we shouldn't grieve because my grandmother wouldn't want us to cry. This concept was foreign to me as I am used to openly grieving. I think that others who look at my culture and the ways in which we grieve may find them foreign and weird. One thing is for sure—I grieve at all funerals. Even if I didn't know the person well, just seeing others grieve makes me cry. All in all, I believe that it is very necessary for some form of ritual to take place when death occurs (Gatling, 2002).

A colleague shares the following:

Once I went to the funeral of a mutual friend, with a friend. The deceased was a Jehovah's Witness, and they conduct memorial services instead of funerals with a body and sermon, as is customary in some other cultures. Well after we were seated, the friend with me asked where the body was, because she had never been to a service where there was no body and people were not crying and becoming very emotional. I politely pointed towards an urn on a pedestal and explained that the body was in the vase. She almost fainted and it was all I could do to contain myself and not burst out laughing. Afterwards she too began to laugh because she now realized that there are different strokes for different people. This person is my best friend and we still laugh about the day she found out what it was like to attend a memorial service at a Kingdom Hall (Walker, 2003).

Many counselors, teachers, and rehabilitation specialists now include spirituality in their assessments and interventions. Just as individual helpers cannot be expected to be competent with all of the multitude of cultural groups found in most practice settings, not all helpers are expected to be experts in spirituality. However, it is useful to be aware of diverse religious and spiritual practices in order to better understand their significance to those we are helping (Holloway, 2002). Inclusive language that uses a variety of religious and spiritual references is important in conveying understanding and acceptance in exploring coping. For example, open-ended questions that acknowledge differences are more helpful than close-ended questions such as, "Are you planning to hold a funeral?" An example of an open-ended question is, "Is there a specific spiritual or religious practice that you or your family have found helpful in the past?" This question conveys understanding that there is wide variation in the practices or beliefs of individuals and families. Familiarity with a broad range of practices and belief systems enables a counselor to better use inclusive language. However, even more important than specific knowledge is the awareness of different cultures and the willingness to acknowledge personal limitations in the knowledge of those cultures and spiritual orientations.

It is also important to attend to verbal and non-verbal signals that might indicate the importance of religion or spirituality. The presence of religious or spiritual articles such as clothing, medals, or books might indicate that the grieving person is drawing on spiritual resources. When concern or conflict about religion or spirituality is expressed by someone facing loss, there may be a need for further exploration or referral to a spiritual resource. There are a number of tools that are used by psychologists, social workers, and pastoral care counselors to assess spirituality.

Pulchalski (1999) has developed a user-friendly tool for assessing the importance of spirituality in people's lives. She notes that FICA is an acronym:

> F: Faith or beliefs
> I: Importance and influence
> C: Community
> A: Address

Some specific questions you can use to discuss each of these issues are:

> F: What is your faith or belief?
>   Do you consider yourself spiritual or religious?
>   What beliefs give meaning to your life?
> I: Is faith important in your life?
>   What influence does your faith have on how you take care of yourself?
>   How have your beliefs influenced your behavior during times of illness?
>   What role do your beliefs play in regaining your health?
> C: Are you part of a spiritual or religious community?
>   Does this community offer support to you and how?
>   Is there a person or group of people you love or who are especially important to you?
> A: Would you prefer your healthcare provider to address issues of faith and belief in your healthcare?
> (Retrieved October 12, 2004 from http://www2.edc.org/lastacts/archives /archivesNov99/assesstool.asp)

Requests for spiritual counseling or expressions of existential doubt are verbal indications of spiritual needs. Sometimes a referral to the hospital chaplain or a resource in your community for pastoral or spiritual counseling is helpful. Many grieving people have already established relationships with pastors or a spiritual practitioner to whom they can turn in times of distress.

As with culture, it is also important when it comes to spirituality not to make assumptions but rather to listen carefully to what an individual or family is expressing, use inclusive language when inquiring about what they find helpful, and be ready to support them, even if the practice may be unfamiliar to you. Joan Ramos (2003) notes that, "There are wide variations across groups in nations of origin, but many cultural beliefs do not separate spiritual or emotional from physical causes of illness. . . . The importance of developing a respectful relationship with patients . . . cannot be overemphasized (p.10)." Additional resources and literature are included in the references and Internet Resources near the end of this chapter.

Exercise: Grief in a Cultural Context _____

Select a movie or video that depicts loss and grief within a specific cultural context. (This exercise includes a list of suggested movies, although you may know of others that are available at your local library or video store). Retail outlets also sell them and provide reviews online. Read the following questions before you watch the movie and be prepared to write your answers or discuss them with others.

1. Discuss the funeral rituals or mourning behavior you have observed.
2. What aspects of these rituals are similar to the practices of your own cultural or religious group?
3. What aspects are different?
4. Of the rituals, practices, or behaviors you have observed in the videos or your own life, which ones do you feel would be particularly helpful for those who have experienced a loss?

Suggested movies: *Soul Food*, *My Girl*, *Ordinary People*, *Smoke Signals*, *Steel Magnolias*, *To Live!*, *Garden State*

(Note: The movies on this list have been chosen for their themes of loss. However, some of the material may elicit unanticipated emotional reactions or may be objectionable to some viewers. You may want to read reviews before making a selection and remember to exercise discretion and self-care in making choices and completing this exercise.)

Self-Test _____

1. Lack of awareness of different cultural groups' responses to loss can lead to which of the following errors:
   a. Misinterpreting an individual's or family's reactions
   b. Failing to offer support or assistance that might be perceived as helpful
   c. Offending the grieving person(s), creating a barrier to their receiving care and support.
   d. All of the above

2. In the 2001 Gallop Poll regarding religion, what percentage of respondents reported that religion is very important?
   a. 15%
   b. 25%
   c. 55%
   d. 95%

   Answers: 1) d   2) c

Internet Resources _____

National Association of Social Work Standards for Cultural Competence can be viewed at
   http://www.socialworkers.org/sections/credentials/cultural_comp.asp
Last Acts has published useful documents on diversity and spirituality in their online journal,
   Innovations in End-of-Life Care at http://www2.edc.org/lastacts/
Specific information on religious beliefs and practices, including those related to death, pertaining to many different ethnic groups is available at http://www.ethnomed.org

The American Association of Family Physicians has published several useful continuing education articles including one that describes a cultural competence continuum and strategies for improvement of one's practice. One article is available at http://www.aafp.org/fpm/20020600/39achi.html

The FICA spiritual assessment tool developed by Christina Puchalski is available at http://www2.edc.org/lastacts/archives/archivesNov99/assesstool.asp

The Georgetown University Center for Child and Human Development has established a Web site for a National Center for Cultural Competence at http://www.georgetown.edu/research/gucdc/nccc/

References

Baron, K. (2003). *Loss and bereavement journal.* Springfield, MA: Springfield College School of Social Work.

Butler-Jones, C. (2003). *Loss and bereavement journal.* Springfield, MA: Springfield College School of Social Work.

Davis, A. (2003). *Loss and bereavement journal.* Springfield, MA: Springfield College School of Social Work.

DeVeux, S. (2002). *Loss and bereavement journal.* Springfield, MA: Springfield College School of Social Work.

Elias, D. (2003). *Loss and bereavement journal.* Springfield, MA: Springfield College School of Social Work.

Fadiman, A. (1998). *The spirit catches you and you fall down: A Hmong child, her American doctors, and the collision of two cultures.* New York: Farrar, Straus & Giroux.

Gatling, R. (2002). *Loss and bereavement journal.* Springfield, MA: Springfield College School of Social Work.

Grollman, E. (1996). Reflections on spiritual problems. *Journeys: Hospice foundation of America newsletter,* April, 1–4.

Highfield, M., & Cason, C. (1983). Spiritual needs of patients: Are they recognized? *Cancer Nursing, 6*(3), 187–192.

Holloway, K. (2002). *Passed on: African American mourning stories.* Durham, NC: Duke University Press.

Irish, D. P., & Lundquist, K. F. (Eds.). (1993). *Ethnic variations in dying, death, and grief.* New York: Taylor and Francis.

Koenig, B., & Gates-Williams, J. (1995). Understanding cultural differences in caring for dying patients. *The Western Journal of Medicine, 163*:245.

NASW Standards for culturally competent practice retrieved on September 1, 2004 from http://www.socialworkers.org/sections/credentials/cultural_comp.asp#intro/

Puchalski, C. (1999). FICA spiritual assessment tool retrieved on January 8, 2004 from http://www.2.edc.org/lastacts/archives/archivesNov99/assesstool.asp/

Ramos, J. (2003). Diversity in cancer care: Focus on Latino patients and families. *Association of oncology social work news, 19*(2), 6,10.

Romer, A. (1999). Taking a spiritual history allows clinicians to understand patients more fully: An interview with Dr. Christina Puchalski. *Innovations in End-of-Life Care, 1*(6), retrieved January 14, 2004 from http://www2.edc.org/lastacts/archives/archivesNov99/featureinn.asp#Puch

Silva, M. (2003). *Loss and bereavement journal.* Springfield, MA: Springfield College School of Social Work.

Tran, D. (2003). *Loss and bereavement journal.* Springfield, MA: Springfield College School of Social Work.

Walker, T. (2003) *Loss and bereavement journal.* Springfield, MA: Springfield College School of Social Work.

6

What Can We Do To Help?

> *Do what you can, with what you have, where you are.*
>
> —Teddy Roosevelt

Misconceptions about Grief

A counseling student writes about her experiences dealing with others' grief:

> A situation which causes me discomfort and that I need to work on is feeling like I am prying when I try to encourage someone to talk to me about their feelings. I have such a strong sense of personal privacy and personal space that I naturally assume others have that sense, and therefore I often feel that asking personal questions is intruding. I realize from reading about grief that often people will not talk about loss and death without encouragement from another person, and even are relieved when someone else brings it up. But it still feels like a risk to bring up difficult issues and encourage those who are grieving to explore their feelings (Kaiser, 2002).

Depending on our own experiences with loss, the cultural norms we have grown up with, and many other factors such as our relationship with the person who is grieving, we may or may not feel comfortable acknowledging a loss and talking with others about their feelings. Because grief results from many different types of losses, not only from death, many different situations can remind people of their losses and trigger a grief reaction. Just as acknowledging loss is an important part of grieving a death, it is also an important part of working through grief related to other losses such as divorce, foster care placement, and even job loss.

Many of us wonder how best to be helpful and acknowledge loss, especially when we are uncertain about the affected person's comfort level or potential reaction to our outreach.

There are many common misconceptions about grief that can inhibit our reaching out to those who are grieving. Not knowing what to do or say, people often avoid acknowledging or talking about a loss to an affected individual or family. Unfortunately, this can lead to a grieving person feeling isolated and alone. The following list includes common misconceptions about grief and provides helpful ways to support yourself and others in making the transition from grief to healing.

- **Misconception 1**: *Time heals all wounds.*
  Time alone does not heal. It is what people do over time that matters. To facilitate healing, people need to be able to acknowledge their loss, express their feelings, and feel a sense of connection with others who care.
- **Misconception 2**: *People find it too painful to talk about their loss.*
  Many people coping with grief have expressed that even though it can be painful at times, they also find it comforting and healing to have opportunities to express and share their feelings in a safe and nurturing environment. This connection provides a source of comfort and strength, thereby creating a foundation for healing to begin.
- **Misconception 3**: *Crying indicates that someone is not coping well.*
  We sometimes feel that tears or other expressions of strong emotions are signs of weakness or a reflection that we are not handling things well. However, these expressions are a normal and healthy response to loss. Friends and interested others can help by being supportive listeners and by encouraging survivors when they feel ready to share these heartfelt emotions.
- **Misconception 4**: *The grieving process should last about one year.*
  There is no designated timeline for how long the grieving process should last. There are no absolutes with grieving. It is important that people process and work through their grief in a way that feels comfortable to them.
- **Misconception 5**: *Quickly putting grieving behind will speed the process of healing.*
  Blocking out or repressing feelings can actually serve as a barrier to healing. Rushing the grieving process is not effective either. Others can help by supporting the need to grieve and actively listening to the thoughts and feelings of those who are grieving and sharing memories.

It may be helpful to know that the literature on grief includes many more reports of people feeling upset that their loss was not acknowledged by others than reports about their losses being too frequently acknowledged. (With the exception of very public losses, such as those related to 9/11.) In fact, when a loss is not acknowledged and support is not offered, survivors may experience disenfranchised grief, a

form of complicated grieving that was discussed in Chapter 4. It is even often important to acknowledge an impending loss, as in the case of a life-limiting illness, since
the affected individual or family member may be experiencing anticipatory grief and
will benefit from support.

A caseworker for children and adolescents in foster care writes:

> A huge part of the treatment with children in a foster care setting is helping them to
> process their feelings about being separated from their loved ones and supporting them
> around these feelings. In many ways it's like a loss through death. The emotions
> expressed by children in out-of-home placements are anger, frustration, sadness, anxi-
> ety, confusion, disbelief, mistrust . . . all of the same emotions that a child would express
> if they were experiencing bereavement from a death. Rando (1984) points out that it is
> important to provide children with constructive ways to address their grief. Doing this
> will also facilitate a working relationship with these children. Validation is a big part of
> the work that I do. I try my best to identify with them and their feelings and validate
> them whenever possible. It is also important in this type of work that all providers are
> on the same page. The therapist, psychiatrist, outreach mentor, teacher, after-school pro-
> gram staff, foster family, birth family, and case worker all need to communicate regu-
> larly and share information. Whenever there is a dilemma involving the client in any
> facet of his or her treatment it is vital for all providers to be aware of it. Intervention and
> structure needs to remain consistent for trust and a healthy working relationship with the
> child (Baron, 2002).

Empathic Communication

Most experts in the fields of both therapeutic communication and grief encourage the
use of basic empathic communication skills in acknowledging a distressing situation
and providing support. These skills are important in all helping situations but are
especially important to practice in the context of grief, when discomfort in one or
both parties may impede the connection.

Rando (1984) describes therapeutic communication in the context of loss as
communication that expresses respect, maintains realistic hope, and offers appropriate reassurance and support through statements of comprehension and empathy.
Empathy involves trying to put ourselves in the other person's shoes and responding
in the way that helps them to feel comfortable, not necessarily with what makes us
feel comfortable. Key skills of empathic communication include active listening and
communication facilitation.

Active listening involves *displaying behavior that indicates we are listening,*
including:

- Appropriate eye contact
- Attentive body language such as leaning forward slightly
- Verbal following (nodding, and verbal statements such as "I see" indicate that
  you are following what the person is saying and interested in hearing it)

Communication facilitation, *a method of encouraging and clarifying conversation*, includes:

- Reflection of feeling ("It sounds like you're feeling really sad.")
- Paraphrasing (Summarizing or repeating in shortened form what was said.)
- Use of minimal encouragers ("Can you tell me a little more?")
- Use of open-ended questions ("How is your sleeping and eating these days?")
- Therapeutic silence (Allowing silence and space in the conversation for thoughts or feelings to emerge.)

The art of reflecting involves restating your understanding of the emotional content of what the person you are listening to is saying, not just their words. In general, when communicating with someone who has experienced a loss it is helpful to avoid the following:

- Saying "I know how you feel" or "I understand."
- Talking about your own losses (me-too-ism).
- Parroting or repeating the speaker's exact words. Try, instead, to respond to the actual content expressed.
- Thinking about or planning your own responses instead of listening to what is being said.
- Giving unsolicited advice.
- Breaking silences too quickly or filling in before the speaker has finished speaking.
- Expressing judgments about what the speaker is saying, such as commenting that they are wise.
- Using clichés.
- Challenging the other person's perception of their situation or feelings.

Case Example

An intuitive special education teacher recently recounted her experience with a child that illustrates the importance of empathic communication. She teaches in a resource room in a large urban magnet school serving grades 1-4. She had been hearing from the second grade teacher about an eight-year-old who was exhibiting defiant behavior in the classroom and who had been involved in several altercations with other children in the class. While he had been a student in the school since kindergarten and had performed well academically in the past, he had recently been placed in foster care due to his mother's inability to care for him. Her health was rapidly failing due to AIDS, and while two younger siblings were placed together in a pre-adoptive home, he was placed in temporary foster care. One day, not long after hearing about this child's classroom behavior, the special education teacher saw him sitting angrily in the principal's office where he had been sent for disciplinary action.

Since the principal was not available, the teacher offered to allow him to wait in her resource room during her lunch break. A simple inquiry, "It sounds like you've been having some pretty rough times?", unleashed a rush of emotions—anger and tears all mixed together. He was angry about being taken from his mother's home and the separation from his siblings, and even more furious about moving to a different foster home each night. Simply reflecting his feelings, "That sounds like it's really hard," led to an outpouring of grief. With hot tears he reported that he could take care of his mother and his little sisters and he was worried that his mom could die because he knew she was really sick. Due to the unavailability of a longer-term foster home, he was being housed each night in a different emergency foster home, each with its own rules, demands, and stresses.

As was discussed earlier, complicated grief can result when loss is not acknowledged and the individual experiencing the loss does not have an opportunity to grieve. It is likely that the empathic listening that the attuned teacher displayed was a key intervention that allowed the overwhelmed little boy to express his acute feelings of grief. The next step would be to alert the school adjustment counselor as well as the protective services caseworker to the intense grief needs he was expressing. This could lead to any number of therapeutic interventions, including individual counseling or play therapy, participation in a peer support group, and the opportunity to participate in art or journaling activities to allow him to express his feelings.

Utilizing Information and Resources

Although the attacks on the World Trade Center and the Pentagon on September 11 of 2001 represent a horrific tragedy for the United States, positive lessons were learned and a wealth of resources were produced in response to this tragedy. As a result, there are many more sources of information and support available now to assist those who are trying to cope with grief and loss. Important ways that a counselor can help, in addition to empathically communicating, include sharing information and utilizing the existing resources provided by experts in grieving. The first step is to be aware of what information and resources are available.

The exercise for the last chapter in this book involves developing your own notebook or file of resources to keep on hand for future reference (if your organization does not already have this available). This includes identifying key experts in your own organization and community and obtaining their contact information. You can then refer to this directory when you, or someone with whom you work, needs assistance. In addition, the Internet resources for this and other chapters are excellent sources of information for both professional helpers and those who are grieving. National organizations like the Compassionate Friends (a support organization for parents who have lost a child) or COPS (an organization assisting survivors of police who die in the line of duty) can be especially helpful to people living in rural areas or people whose unique losses may not be as common in their local community.

Who has expertise that you can tap?

Many schools and organizations employ social workers, psychologists, or other counselors who have expertise in grief counseling and who can be called upon for leadership and guidance when needed. Businesses often have Employee Assistance Programs (EAP) that provide consultation to employees on a variety of issues. Some of these programs provide counseling and educational resources or referrals to programs in your community.

If expertise is not available in your organization, or if additional assistance is needed, most communities have hospice organizations or family counseling agencies where expertise is readily available. A directory of hospice locations is available on the Web sites of the National Hospice and Palliative Care Organization and the National Hospice Foundation. Many communities now have centers for grief and loss or other specialized programs that provide consultation. Some of these, such as The Dougy Center and The Front Porch have Web sites that offer a wealth of information in addition to direct services. Other organizations, such as Cancer Care, offer online consultation or support to individuals and groups. Caution must be exercised, of course, in referring to any provider. Evidence of professional training and appropriate licensure of staff should be listed in the organizational information of reputable providers. Generally this training requires an MD, PhD or master's degree in social work, psychology, educational counseling, pastoral care, or other related human service professions. Peer support can be invaluable but some evidence of professional consultation or supervision is generally a requirement for organizations that wish to protect and support clients in need. A list of selected links that have been carefully reviewed are included in the Internet resources near the end of this chapter.

Collaborating with Others

The value of teamwork is emphasized in most professional training programs today, and is especially important in complex situations such as those involving grief. In most settings, including schools, medical, correctional, and child and family service agencies, members of an interdisciplinary team are responsible for helping to carry out educational or therapeutic goals. Whether formally "teaming" to construct an Individualized Educational Plan (IEP) in a school setting or informally consulting with other members of the team in a rehabilitation setting, team members are usually responsible for certain core functions related to goal attainment. These include:

- Completing a thorough assessment
- Contributing to the development of a comprehensive educational/treatment plan
- Participating as a member of the interdisciplinary team
- Implementing the components of the educational/treatment plan
- Evaluating progress
- Advocating

Each member of the interdisciplinary team has expertise that they bring to the assessment and planning process and each can play an important role in assisting with grief-related issues. Teachers often identify grief issues when they are reflected in their students' written assignments or in their behavior. The physician, physician's assistant, and nurse practitioner often identify unresolved or masked grief that may be expressed by a patient through somatic complaints or requests for sleeping pills or other medications. When a chaplain is a member of the team, he or she can carry out a spiritual assessment and treatment plan. The benefits of a spiritual perspective are reflected in Rabbi Harold Kusher's book *When Bad Things Happen to Good People* (2004). The rehabilitation specialists on the team, including occupational and physical therapists and speech-language pathologists, carry out essential roles in helping to assess functional capacities and can make a significant contribution in referring those whose complicated grief reactions may be, in Worden's (2002) terms, exaggerated or chronic.

Functions of Team Members

Social workers, psychologists, and educational counselors are generally responsible for assessing psychosocial and emotional needs and recommending or carrying out treatment plans to address these, including supportive counseling to aid in adjustment to loss. An understanding of the risk factors and interventions associated with complicated and unresolved grief is a key contribution of these disciplines to the team. Another area of expertise that these team members contribute is an understanding of **compassion fatigue** or secondary trauma (Figley, 1995). These terms describe *the reactions that professional caregivers sometimes experience in the process of helping others with grief, loss, and trauma.* Compassion fatigue may occur when a professional helper's own emotional resources become depleted. This can happen when professionals don't have an opportunity to process their grief or when their exposure to grief and loss is prolonged. **Secondary trauma** refers to the *trauma that professional caregivers can experience through listening to the details of trauma that others have experienced.* This is also sometimes referred to as **vicarious trauma**.

The same strategies that are useful in helping family members cope with loss are also useful in helping professionals cope effectively with the demands of their work. These strategies include expressing feelings to others who can listen empathically and provide support. This sometimes takes place in team debriefing sessions, in individual supervision or consultation, or through staff support programs. Other strategies include routinely using stress management techniques and making sure there is a balance in our lives through exercising and taking vacation or respite when we are feeling fatigued or distressed.

Interdisciplinary team collaboration benefits everyone because members of each discipline contribute their specialized expertise to the treatment or education plan and team members can support each other as they work their way through losses. While some team members provide more direct counseling than others, each member must also be prepared to understand and respond effectively to the various types of distress expressed by both colleagues and clients. This is particularly true in situations involving grief when the client or student has a strong relationship with a particular professional. The client might feel more comfortable disclosing their feelings of sadness, anxiety, or anger to a specific teacher or coach. In this kind of relationship the school adjustment counselor can serve as a consultant to the primary helper. It is also important for everyone on the team to be aware of situations in which feelings are being expressed indirectly through acting out or withdrawal from peers or social interaction. In some cases, a person who is grieving a loss may be receiving services for another identified problem but disclose their feelings related to the loss to the physical therapist, nurse, or teacher who is working with them on a daily basis. Using basic empathic communication skills, everyone can listen supportively and help problem-solve when emotional distress is evident. And everyone can make significant contributions to individuals and families through making appropriate referrals. Directly providing social support that is needed by those grieving a loss is something every helper can offer. Margaret Drench provides many examples of how rehabilitation professionals can provide support in her online continuing education course on loss, grief, and adjustment offered by the American Physical Therapy Association Web site. In discussing situations such as a woman evidencing grief while participating in rehabilitation following a spinal cord injury, and another woman whose movement is impaired due to Parkinson's Disease, she notes:

> Although counseling is beyond the boundaries of physical therapist practice, physical therapists need to use skills—such as listening and the ability to acknowledge the concerns, beliefs, and fears of patients and clients—and display a caring demeanor. The physical therapist can offer pragmatic suggestions that focus on outcomes of physical independence and self-esteem, which might diminish their patients' sense of isolation and help them adjust to their losses (Drench, 2003, p. 5).

Like the American Physical Therapy Association, professional organizations in every discipline have developed information to help other professionals and the public to understand their areas of expertise. These organizations also provide resources and guidance to their members about specific areas of practice, such as end of life care or crisis intervention. The National Association of Social Work, for example, has outlined the roles and functions of social workers in different arenas of practice and articulates the values of the profession in its code of ethics (www. naswdc.org). NASW has also recently developed standards of practice for social workers in end of life care. The American Academy of Physician Assistants has published policy papers on various aspects of the physician's assistant role that include information on communicating around end of life issues. In addition, AAPA has developed clinical practice guidelines in which the team approach is promoted. "The team approach to the practice of medicine certainly enhances communication, efficiency, and patient care" (AAPA, 2004). Other professional organizations include the American Occupational Therapy Association and the National Education Association (NEA), which is a professional organization for teachers. NEA offers several very useful resources for educators on their Web site including a crisis tool that is designed to assist teachers, administrators, and school personnel. The tool provides an overview of children's concepts of death as well as strategies for schools following the death of a student. Excellent curricula and resources are available through the project Web sites of ELNEC (End-of-Life Nursing Education Consortium) and EPEC (Education on Palliative and End-of-Life Care).

The Web sites of these and other professional organizations offer a variety of publications and resources that can aid you, and the families you serve, in understanding and accessing the services these disciplines provide. An example is an article in the *Magazine of the Society for Human Resource Management* entitled "Helping Employees Cope With Grief" (Tyler, 2003), published on the SHRM Web site. This article not only provides guidance for the human resource professional, but also links to other organizations and Web articles on the topic of grief and loss.

Exercise: Active Listening

This exercise is very useful and is recommended by many counselors—not only for grief work but also for couples who want to improve their communication, and for co-workers on busy interdisciplinary teams.

Choose a partner. Both of you will have a chance to be the listener and the speaker, but decide who will speak first and who will listen. (You will then switch.)

1. The first speaker talks for five minutes. Because the topic of this chapter is communicating about grief, you may decide that you will both talk about "talking about death." If you are doing the exercise in another context, the speaker can choose any topic(s) he or she wishes to talk about.
2. While the speaker talks, the listener practices active listening, using only non-verbal communication. (Making appropriate eye contact, leaning forward, nodding, etc.) The listener should not speak. When five minutes has passed, the listener then repeats back everything that the speaker said. It is important to try to say just what the speaker said, with no editorial comments or evaluations, and, in general, in the same tone and manner.
3. When the listener has finished repeating back what was said, talk together about the conversation. Discuss the following questions:
   - How did it feel to you as the speaker to have someone fully listening to you?
   - How did it feel to hear what you said repeated back to you?
   - How comfortable was it for you as the listener to listen silently? How did it help or hinder your efforts to listen?
4. Now reverse roles and repeat the exercise and the discussion, with the initial speaker doing the listening.
5. Finally, discuss what the conversation was like in your new roles.
   - Was it more challenging or rewarding for you to be in the listener role or the speaker role?
   - How might you use what you've learned from this exercise in the future?

Self-Test

1. Which of the following is NOT a therapeutic communication skill in the context of grief?

    a. Attending behavior
    b. Reflection of feeling
    c. Silence
    d. Telling someone about our own losses

2. Which of the following is NOT a common misconception about grief?
    a. Expression of feelings related to grief is helpful
    b. People find it too painful to talk about a loss
    c. Crying indicates that someone is not coping well with loss
    d. Time heals all wounds

Answers: 1) d   2) a

Internet Resources

"The 3 V's of Good Friendship: Supporting Your Friend Through Illness and Loss" and other articles published by the Hospice Foundation of America can be found at http://www.hospicefoundation.org/

The American Association of Physician Assistants has published a policy on end of life care on its Web site at http://www.aapa.org/policy/end-of-life.html

The American Physical Therapy Association offers continuing education material on grief at http://www.apta.org

The American Occupational Therapy Association Web site can be found at http://www.aota.org

The National Education Association (and affiliated state teachers' associations) offers helpful information for teachers and school administrators at http://www.nea.org/crisis

Guidelines and interventions for grief are included in the End-of-Life Nursing Education Consortium (ELNEC) curriculum at http://www.aacn.nche.edu/ELNEC/index.htm and the Education on Palliative and End-of-Life Care (EPEC) project of the Northwestern University Feinberg School of Medicine at http://epec.net/EPEC/webpages/index.cfm

References

American Association of Physician Assistants. (2004). *Clinical practice guidelines.* Alexandria, VA: American Association of Physician Assistants.

Baron, K. (2002). *Loss and bereavement journal.* Springfield, MA: Springfield College School of Social Work.

Drench, M. E. (2004). Loss, grief, and adjustment: A primer for physical therapy, Parts I & II. *APTA continuing education series,* no. 27. Alexandria, VA: American Physical Therapy Association.

Figley, C. (1995). *Compassion fatigue: Coping with secondary traumatic stress disorder in those who treat the traumatized.* New York: Brunner-Routledge.

Kaiser, L. (2002). *Loss and bereavement journal.* Springfield, MA: Springfield College School of Social Work.

Kushner, H. J. (2004). *When bad things happen to good people.* (Twentieth Anniversary Ed.). New York: Anchor Books.

Rando, T. (1984). *Grief, dying and death: Clinical interventions for caregivers.* Champaign, IL: Research Press Company.

Tyler, K. (2003). Helping employees cope with grief. *HRMagazine, 48*(9). Retrieved January 3, 2004 from http://www.shrm.org/hrmagazine/articles/0903/0903tyler.asp

Worden, W. (2002). *Grief counseling and grief therapy: A handbook for the mental health practitioner.* (3rd ed.). New York: Springer Publishing.

7

When Organizations and Communities Grieve

> *As the sun illuminates the moon and stars so let us illuminate each other.*
>
> —Master Lui

Grief experts identify many ways in which memorial ceremonies, rituals, and activities assist those who are grieving. Funerals and memorial activities validate the lives of those who are deceased and can strengthen the connections of those who survive losses. Family and friends are reminded of the importance of every life—the deceased's as well as their own—during funerals and commemorative activities. As discussed in earlier chapters, issues related to grief and loss are present not only in cases of death but also in symbolic losses. Many people have developed rituals and ceremonies to grieve symbolic losses such as divorces or moving from one's place of origin. Harry Close, a pastoral counselor, has published a book entitled *Ceremonies for Healing and Growth* that includes a ritual of transition for leaving one's home for a nursing home, and a ceremony for divorce. In the divorce ceremony, Close begins by stating, "We are here today with sadness, to bear witness to the painful side of our human existence. . .we here today stand with you in your grieving, to affirm our ties with you, our support for you in this anxious time of transition and rebuilding (p. 43)." Like all rituals, the ceremonies for special situations assist those who are grieving by providing an opportunity for the acknowledgment and expression of feelings

85

related to the loss. Providing practical and emotional support before, during, and after these activities is a way that members of a support network or community can express their caring. Sometimes, a ritual of remembrance or a memorial ceremony can help bring closure and convey support for unresolved losses even years after the actual loss.

Case Example

Tim, a case worker in a group home for teenagers in therapeutic foster care, was concerned about a client who was left without any direct family connections after his grandmother's death. The client, T.C., who was 16, had initially lived with his grandmother after his mother's death but had been in foster care for several years after his grandmother's illness made it impossible for her to care for him. After his grandmother died, T.C. asked to visit the family gravesite. The group home staff learned that there was no gravestone to mark the site where T.C.'s mother and grandmother were buried because of inadequate finances. T.C. expressed distress about the absence of a gravestone and began to save money to purchase one. The therapeutic staff believed that it might help T.C. to complete the tasks of grieving if he could accomplish this, but they knew it would take him a very long time, since he earned only minimum wage at his part-time job.

The residents and staff of the group home joined T.C.'s efforts to raise money by collecting beverage cans and redeeming them for the cash deposit value. Many neighboring families and businesses in the community were made aware of the endeavor and contributed their bottles and cans. This activity helped T.C. to purchase a gravestone to memorialize his family in a way that was meaningful to him, provided him with a location and mechanism for remembering his family, and increased the outreach and social support he received from others.

If attuned to unresolved loss, most community professionals can identify loss-related needs in every aspect of their work. The members of the community in the group home case example chose to respond to an expressed need through collective efforts to help T.C. achieve his goal of memorializing a loved one. The many types of losses that children, teens, and adults experience, and that we will encounter through our interactions with them, present both challenges and opportunities for professionals to be helpful. Counselors can make a significant difference through a variety of helpful responses:

- Practicing empathic communication, as discussed in Chapter 6.
- Referring a client to a support group, a bereavement counselor, or another community provider, as discussed in Chapter 4, is sometimes the best type of help we can provide.

- Attending a funeral or planning a memorial service can serve as an expression of support to surviving family members and can also assist us, as professional helpers, to cope with our own grief in reaction to a loss.
- Offering to be present with those who are grieving as they express their feelings or carry out rituals of remembrance.

Just as it is important to assess our own motives and skills when addressing grief that we suspect is causing distress, it is also important to assess our motives as well as the impact our actions will have on the person who is grieving when we are deciding whether or not to attend a funeral or memorial service. In many instances clients or students are comforted by the presence of familiar professionals at important public ceremonies of remembrance. Some helping professionals have also attended funerals or memorials to show their respect to the family of the person who has died and to acknowledge their own grief. A medical social worker writes:

> Both Therese Rando and William Worden speak to the benefits accorded an individual through the funeral ritual. Because there are varying degrees of involvement that I have with each patient and family member I see, I would not, nor would I feel the need to, attend the service of every patient who dies. There are, however, patients, for whatever reason, that I become close with, who touch my heart, who teach me and who I am better for having known. For those patients, the grief I feel at their death is very real. In a hospital environment where one often needs to be readily available to go from one situation to the next, feelings about the losses that occur have to be put on hold and remain there for some time to come. The funeral ritual provides for me a place to reflect upon and grieve the loss, pay tribute to the individual, acknowledge the importance of the loss to the family, and let the family know their loved one made a difference in my life (Jaycox, 2003).

While professionals' attendance at memorials can be very helpful to family members, depending on the relationship with the survivors, there are also times when a professional helper's presence might be uncomfortable for the individual or family who has sustained a loss. As with other grief interventions, the decision to attend a service or ceremony planned by a grieving family should always be based on an assessment of how it will meet the grieving individual's or family's needs rather than our own. Except in very large public ceremonies or services, such as a city-wide memorial service for a public servant killed in the line of duty, we must always think carefully about why we should or should not attend and if it will serve the needs of the client for us to remain absent. There are many other ways to attend to our own grief reactions, including debriefing or processing in a team meeting or agency-sponsored memorial.

Taking a Leadership Role

There are also situations that call for all professionals, as members of a larger organization or community, to join together to support one another, and those they serve, in coping with a loss. You have most likely heard about or participated in such efforts. You may, in the future, find yourself taking a leadership role in helping your organization or community provide guidance and support to others. The situations discussed on page ix of the Preface to this book are examples.

The first example concerned a faculty member at a college who died just before the close of the school year. The department head called together administrators from each discipline, along with a grief consultant, to create and implement a plan. In a community or a larger organization such as a private corporation or public service agency there are usually many resources that can be utilized for this kind of consultation and planning. Counseling staff, school guidance professionals, and employee assistance personnel often have expertise in grief. In an academic setting, the college chaplain is often a source of support and guidance. There may be faculty in college and university departments who have expertise they can share, and students and staff who have experience in coping with grief or who are motivated to help gather information and resources. Usually all that is needed to put together a response team in an organization is an individual who takes responsibility for contacting administrative personnel from the relevant departments or employee groups, as well as someone with expertise on grief responses.

Most communities have mental health agencies or professionals with expertise in grief who can be called upon to assist in a crisis if there is not an expert within the organization. Once an organization has been through such a process a protocol is usually established that can be implemented any time a death or major loss occurs.

Establishing a Bereavement Protocol: Interdisciplinary and Inter-Organizational Collaboration

Here are some steps that organizations can take following a loss to help those affected:

1. First, communicate the news to all the members of the school or organizational community who knew the deceased. This is often done through electronic bulletin boards, letters distributed in mail boxes, and personalized phone calls to those who may have a close connection. A sensitively worded statement can be made such as, "It is with deep sadness that we inform you of the death of one of our community members . . ." This will serve to inform people of the death and can also be a vehicle for disseminating information about funeral or memorial services. It may be important to provide the contact number for a counseling service, chaplain, or a crisis service in the message for those who may need to talk with someone personally.

2. Provide concrete ways for people to express their caring and concern. In many organizational and academic settings students and staff have spontaneously created memorials by placing flowers, pictures, poems, and notes of remembrance

in a foyer or outside an office. Notes of remembrance often describe memorable moments in the classroom or office, or significant interactions with the person who has died. These recollections might then be collected and recorded in the time leading up to a memorial service where the life and contributions of the faculty member, student, or staff member are honored. Announce the loss in a meeting or class session with time allotted for discussion.

3. Acknowledge the loss in meetings or classes. Publish an article in the school or organization's newsletter, include content on grief and loss in classroom instruction or in-service education programs, and provide small group sessions for anyone wishing to talk about the loss. These are all strategies that model healthy coping and may be considered important life lessons. A similar protocol might be used following tragedies that affect whole communities, like those that occurred on 9/11.

4. Obtain consultation or support for staff who are providing grief counseling to others, if needed.

In the second example in the Preface to this text, a counselor in an alternative high school died after being stabbed in a classroom in front of his students. Interns from our social work program who were at the school took a leadership role in creating a giant mural dedicated to this man and posting it along a central corridor of the school. The mural was quickly filled with hundreds of messages from students and staff. Some chose to write memories, some wrote words of encouragement to his family and others suffering from his loss. The interns and other counselors were positioned close by and were available to provide support and crisis intervention to those who needed it throughout the weeks and months following the tragedy. School administrators and counseling staff communicated with teachers, students, and their families and made arrangements with the school bus transport company so that every student and staff member who wished to could attend the memorial service. Classroom discussions and assignments also provided students with opportunities to express their thoughts and feelings and to memorialize this important person in their lives.

In a local elementary school a memorial "tree" was painted on mural paper and affixed to the wall outside the school office for a month after the death of a beloved school secretary. Students, staff, and parents were invited to write their thoughts on sticky notes and post them on the tree, which was later given to the secretary's family. Teachers offered students time to write poems or draw pictures of the secretary, or anyone else who had died that they wanted to remember, and the school social workers and guidance counselors visited classrooms to acknowledge the loss. Those who expressed distress or appeared to need help coping with the loss were offered small group or individual opportunities to talk.

Another example was provided by a local high school in the community where I reside. An automobile accident took the life of a teenager in the junior class just two days before the senior class graduation. The school administration responded immediately by communicating with one another, the teenager's family, and key members of the school community who knew the student. By the time school opened the following morning, they had implemented a plan. A memorial display was created in the entrance foyer and school personnel greeted all students entering the building with the news and an invitation to view and contribute to the memorial display. They also announced that a memorial service would be held in the school that evening and students interested in participating were encouraged to speak with the guidance counselor. Counseling staff were available throughout the day and evening to provide support to students, and many teachers provided students with opportunities to talk about their reactions during classes.

School and community groups in which the student had participated were actively engaged in planning the memorial service, and a program was quickly put together that included readings and presentations by members of each of these groups, including a performing arts group and the school's chorus. Songs, prayers, and remembrances were created and shared by many different members of the school community. All of these activities served to bring together members of the school and community to support one another. The service also provided a tribute that the student's parents could share in and remember. The timing of this memorial was important as it allowed the loss of the student's life to be acknowledged and honored before the school community proceeded with the senior class graduation.

Each of these examples displays how a small group of committed professionals in a school or organization, with the right support and resources, can take a leadership role in organizing and carrying out an appropriate ritual of remembrance. These examples also show how teamwork can work very effectively, even if the members of the team do not have grief expertise. What is most often required is a pooling of resources and areas of strength, and a commitment to helping each other in the face of tragedy.

Creating Remembrances and Memorials

As a grief counselor, I have often been inspired by the creative and caring rituals that families, communities, and organizations have used to honor and remember loved ones. One group of friends created a memorial cookbook, using the recipes that their dear friend, an avid cook, had served to them before she died. These dishes were prepared and served at her memorial service, accompanied by notes recalling the events and celebrations during which their friend had served them.

A family with whom I am acquainted gathered at a park where their father had enjoyed his daily walks, and then walked along the perimeter together while recalling stories of his life. They then chose a site, overlooking a pond, on which to locate a memorial bench which they donated to the park. Another family I know, who owns a small business, has planted ornamental shrubs on their business property, with small plaques honoring employees who have died and who will be remembered. Many families choose to donate the organs of a deceased family member as a "living tribute" to a loved one. The gratitude and appreciation of life expressed by many recipients during and after a memorial can offer a source of comfort and hope in the face of overwhelming grief.

In the Unity Camp program for families affected by AIDS that takes place at Paul Newman's Double H Camp in Luzerne, NY, an annual ritual has been established to memorialize loved ones. The ritual consists of each family constructing a memorial boat together, made from items they find in the natural environment. The memorial boat is then launched in an evening ceremony. Stories and memories are shared as the family members gather sticks, leaves, bark, and nut shells to decorate their boats, which symbolize the passing on of their loved ones. Later in the evening, just after sunset, each family lights a candle, places it on their boat, and launches the boat onto the lake before gathering around a campfire for shared gospel music (Itin, 2004).

Many hospitals, churches, and community organizations now host an annual memorial service to honor staff and members of the communities they serve who have died. Each year thousands of people walk in the American Cancer Society's Relay for Life to raise money for cancer research and programs. The relay includes a "luminaria lap" during which individuals and families light candles in decorated luminaria bags and walk in memory of their loved ones. Similar events sponsored by other organizations offer a therapeutic means to remember loved ones and make a meaningful contribution to organizations that help others. December 5th has been established as a world-wide annual night of remembrance for parents who have lost a child. Many communities sponsor a gathering for grieving parents to come together on this night to light candles together and remember their children. The public show of support and acknowledgment that these events provide can be invaluable in helping individuals or families connect with one another, acknowledge their feelings, and make meaning of one of life's most difficult experiences—the death of someone important.

While many people rely exclusively on clergy or spiritual community leaders to plan memorial services or events, many books and Web sites now provide guidelines and resources that aid in planning and carrying out these kinds of events as well as information about how to become involved in those that already exist. Musical selections appropriate to the occasion, inspirational readings and quotations, art work for printed programs, and even guidelines for obituaries and eulogies can now be found quite easily, using the resources listed near the end of this chapter.

Service activities represent another arena of memorial interventions that can help to facilitate healthy adaptation after a loss. As noted in Chapter 4, sometimes grieving individuals and communities, particularly those affected by public tragedies, gain a sense of empowerment and hope after devastating loss through actions that help others in some way. Each year hundreds of thousands of individuals throughout the United States walk, run, or bike in memory of loved ones in events like the American Cancer Society's Relay for Life, the Leukemia and Lymphoma Society's Light the Night walk, and the Susan G. Komen Foundation's Race for the Cure.

Additionally, *For the Love of Ali* (Waldsmith, 2000) recounts how Anna Ling Pierce has gained hope and provided inspiration through Ali and Dad's Army, an organization that raises funds for a pediatric cancer treatment center at the University of Massachusetts in honor of her daughter and husband. Ann Pierce's daughter, Ali, died of cancer at age 13 in 1995. Ann's husband and Ali's father, John, created a fundraising organization called Ali's Army to raise money in her memory, and set a goal of raising $500,000 over five years. In October of 1997, just eleven months after Ali's death, John, age 50, died of a heart attack while training with Ali's Army to run and raise money in the Boston Marathon. Ann, while shattered by the loss of her husband and daughter, has found meaning and comfort through continuing Ali and Dad's Army and reaching the $500,000 goal in just one year. She says that she now wakes each day with a crystal clear purpose and feels like she has a family of thousands—the thousands of people who have joined her in raising money for this memorial fund.

While not every family or community will choose to carry out this kind of service or memorial activity following loss, as helping professionals it is important to remember that there are many ways to acknowledge and express both grief and caring. Fortunately, there are many routes and resources to support a diverse array of needs.

I hope that the information and resources included in this chapter, along with the theories and skills discussed throughout the text, will aid you in providing support, comfort, and assistance to the people you encounter who are grieving. Additional resources for designing and implementing interventions to assist communities can be found on the companion Web site for this text. The exercise in this chapter is designed to help you integrate the information you have gathered and put into action a plan for the future.

> *Never doubt that a small group of thoughtful, committed citizens can change the world. Indeed, it is the only thing that ever has.*
>
> —Margaret Mead

Exercise: Mapping a Grief Protocol for Your Organization

1. Review the four tasks of mourning outlined in Worden's model on page 49.
2. Identify the types of potential losses that might impact your organization/community.
3. Develop a plan to identify key people in your organization who might be involved in communicating and decision-making should a loss occur.
4. Develop an agenda for a planning meeting that would be held immediately following a loss and identify who would attend.
5. Develop a communication plan to disseminate information about a loss to members of the organization who might be affected.
6. Develop a list of expert consultants in your community who could assist your organization in responding to a loss (e.g., crisis counselors, hospice or death education programs that could provide consultation, chaplains or other experts in memorial services who could assist in planning). Include their contact information.
7. Identify what role you would feel best equipped to fill in response to a loss within your organization or community.
8. Develop a resource notebook or file with relevant information and models that could be useful in the event of a loss and store it in an easily accessible location for future use.

Self-Test

1. In order to plan an appropriate memorial or remembrance, an organization must have a team of specially trained grief experts.

   _____ True _____ False

2. A bereavement protocol is a series of steps that an organization carries out in response to a death or major loss.

   _____ True _____ False

Answers:

1) False, what is needed is an individual with initiative who takes on the responsibility of contacting administrators and gathering relevant planners.

2) True, a bereavement protocol is a series of steps an organization carries out in response to a death or major loss.

Internet Resources

The National Education Association has developed crisis tools for schools that include descriptions of the roles of school personnel in managing a crisis, templates for school phone trees, and many other useful resources that can be found at http://www.nea.org/crisis/

The Hospice Foundation of America provides excellent resources that can be downloaded and distributed to those who are grieving or to those assisting people who are grieving. Articles on their Web site include: "Facing Sudden Loss" by Judy Tatelbaum, MSW, "Helping a Child Deal with Death" by Nancy Boyd Webb, DSW, and "Grieving" by Kenneth J. Doka, PhD, http://www.hospicefoundation.org

The American Association of Retired Persons (AARP) Web site provides resources including these articles: "Ways to Remember" at http://www.aarp.org/griefandloss/articles/82_a.html and "Practical Matters" at http://www.aarp.org/griefandloss/practical.html

The Center on Aging at the University of Kansas offers a free funeral planning booklet at http://www2.kumc.edu/coa/Info_OlderAdultFam/FuneralBoolet.htm

References

Close, H. T. *Ceremonies for healing and growth.* Atlanta, GA: Self-published.

Itin, C., McFeaters, S., & Taylor-Brown, S. (2004). The family unity program for HIV-affected families: Creating a family-centered and community-building context for interventions. In J. Berzoff & P. Silverman (Eds.), *Living with dying: A handbook for end-of-life care practitioners.* New York: Columbia University Press.

Jaycox, K. (2003). *Loss and bereavement journal.* Springfield, MA: Springfield College School of Social Work.

Waldsmith, L. (2000). For the love of Ali. *Reader's Digest,* February, 78-85.

8

Self-Care: Sustaining Hope, Helpfulness, and Competence in Working with Grief

> *Look well into thyself. There is a source of strength which will always spring up if thou will always look there.*
>
> —Marcus Aurelius

Continuing Education

Professional development encompasses not only the education and training that prepares us for our work with others, but also the ongoing development of knowledge and skills to carry out our work effectively in an ever-changing environment. If you have read this text as part of a professional training program, you will now be better prepared to identify and address grief-related issues as they arise in your work. It will always be important, however, to regularly evaluate your knowledge and skills and to participate in continuing education to remain effective.

Most professionals find continuing education to be essential for many reasons. Continuing education helps to infuse our practice or teaching with new information and methods. Acquiring new knowledge and skills, especially through interaction and contact with other professionals, provides a mechanism for capacity building, consultation, and even support for many who work with challenging and vulnerable populations. Most professional groups recognize the importance of continuing education (CE) and require that professionals participate in CE programs in order to gain, or maintain, licenses or other credentials that ensure competence.

There are many methods for continuing education and advancing professional knowledge and skills. Most academic training programs based in colleges and universities offer courses, advanced certificate programs, or lectures to their alumni and others in topic areas of specific interest to their professional discipline. It is helpful to be aware of the offerings of your college or training program while you are still a student so that you can take advantage of these after you complete your initial training. Professional organizations also offer a wide variety of continuing education options to members as well as the public. It is usually easy to learn what conferences, courses, or even journal articles and newsletters are available to professionals in a particular discipline by conducting an Internet search using your profession's formal title, or by visiting the Web sites of the professional organizations within your discipline.

Conferences and workshops hold special appeal for professionals who are looking for an interactive method of instruction or professional support. Many symposiums and training sessions are conducted every day in different regions of the U.S. and abroad. Some are aimed at a specific discipline such as education or social work, and many professionals find it very helpful to gather with others in their field to discuss issues such as how to assist individuals who are grieving within their own professional roles. Sometimes, because of staffing patterns, or because of the characteristics of an organization, it may be difficult to find others in one's own immediate work setting who share an interest in grief or who have special expertise in this area. Conferences or workshops can provide important discipline-specific information as well as a link to others with similar interests and roles.

Many other continuing education programs are designed to meet the common interests and needs of a multidisciplinary audience. In fact, there is an increasing emphasis on interdisciplinary continuing education in the area of end of life and grief care. These types of symposiums or training sessions include presentations by experts from different perspectives and opportunities for discussion among the various disciplines represented in the audience. Teachers, for example, may find it useful to attend a training session on children's grief with guidance counselors or grief therapists who can discuss specific intervention strategies that can be used in school settings. Corrections officers may find it useful to learn and interact with rehabilitation or substance abuse counselors because the populations they work with may present common clinical problems.

Other professionals may prefer the more in-depth training that a graduate course or an advanced training program offers. Graduate programs often offer postbaccalaureate or post-master's courses and certificate programs to professionals for CE credit. These programs, like symposiums or workshops, offer the opportunity to interact with expert faculty and other professionals and provide a type of built-in consultation and support network that can be invaluable for ongoing professional development, even after the course or program has been completed (Cskai, 2005).

The Internet is also an excellent source of continuing education in the topic areas of trauma, grief, and loss. Many universities, professional organizations, and independent providers of continuing education offer distance-learning options for professionals and the public, which are both cost-effective and efficient. Many of the examples in this text are written by students in a distance-learning section of a course in loss and grief offered through the Springfield College Masters of Social Work program. While some students initially wondered whether a course taught on the Internet could adequately address the topic of grief and loss and meet their professional needs, most have highly recommended the course to others. Internet-based courses and consultation forums, when carefully constructed and monitored by professionals, can provide a measure of privacy that many people appreciate.

An asynchronous Internet discussion allows participants to read each other's entries without the need for everyone to be online at the same time. (An asynchronous discussion is a bulletin board type of discussion, which allows participants to post their responses at times of the day or week that work for them. The postings then can be read by all of the participants in their own time frame.) Busy professionals often find this type of continuing education option efficient both in terms of cost and time. The format also allows the participants to reflect on their thoughts and feelings in private, outside of a classroom or workshop, where some people may feel pressured. Sources of continuing education can be found in the Internet Resources for this chapter as well as on the companion Web site for this course.

Self-Care Strategies

As discussed in Chapter 2, it is also very important for professionals who work closely with people experiencing grief to recognize that they may experience vicarious trauma, grief, and loss through their work. Developing strategies for self-care is an essential component of ongoing professional development that can sustain counselors and help them to avoid **compassion fatigue,** or burn-out when engaged with people who are distressed. **Compassion fatigue** describes *the emotional depletion that professional caregivers may experience when an imbalance occurs in self-care and care for others* (Pfifferling, 2000). A sign of compassion fatigue is when a previously caring and compassionate professional expresses a lack of concern, understanding, or compassion for others who are distressed. A professional who is experiencing compassion fatigue or burn-out may be irritable or express anger when asked to help, make disdainful or negative remarks about a client's distress, or avoid discussing another person's painful feelings because the professional cannot bear to hear one more painful story.

Even when we are well prepared educationally, are self-aware, and have addressed our own past issues with death, trauma, and loss, we can still experience compassion fatigue when working with others who are grieving. It is helpful to have ongoing strategies to create a balance in our lives and to gain support for ourselves as we provide support to others. Yet for many this is easier said than done. For most professionals regular time off is essential, but they may often find it difficult to take vacation or mental health days. Creative expression through art, music, or dance can also be very helpful, yet in a recent training for teachers and school guidance personnel that I attended, most of the seasoned participants lamented that they are so exhausted at the end of the day or work week that they simply can't find the energy or time to meet their own needs for creative expression.

It is a recognized limitation in many professional training programs and contemporary workplaces that professionals' own self-care needs are neglected. Rando (1984) acknowledges that organizational attitudes and policies often contradict what we know contributes to effective practice. She notes:

> Another source of stress is the lack of organizational support that frequently occurs in human service systems: no opportunities for emotional debriefing; unrealistic expectations for support from other staff members, especially those in key roles; no explicit recognition of the need to incorporate meeting staff needs into the schedule (p. 438).

Durfee (2004), the physician cited in Chapter 1 who has written about grief related to child abuse and death due to family violence, also points to the lack of organizational policies and programs that address the grief of child protection and emergency care workers who assist children and families after a case of severe abuse or violent death. He writes, "Almost no intervention is provided to professionals and volunteer service providers who are affected by such a death. An exception may be a Critical Incident Debriefing in one agency, or a supervisor who can balance the employees' need for empathy and protection with the need to feel competent and to continue work." He also points out that while peer support is generally deemed to be helpful, there is rarely time or structure allocated by agencies for this, and protocols are not generally established for provision of staff support or attendance at funerals.

Both Rando and Durfee recommend that organizations take steps to meet the grief related needs of professional caregivers that include opportunities for debriefing and time off, as well as providing education on the grief related needs of clients and workers.

Time off, debriefing, and opportunities for creative expression related to professional caregiver grief are only a few of the many strategies that can sustain us in our work and help us to be most effective. Dale Larson (1993), in his book *The Helper's Journey,* suggests that professional caregivers compartmentalize their work and personal life. "Stress from work can easily spill over into your personal life, and conversely, your private life can be more stressful than your work life. To achieve this success, it is important to put psychological and physical distance between your work life and your home life" (p. 83). In addition to the strategies listed above, many professionals find that their own spiritual practices enable them to find hope and make meaning in the face of loss. And, of course, it is important to practice what we preach and get regular physical exercise, adequate sleep, and follow a nutritionally sound diet.

While this chapter may give you ideas about how the organizations you work for can more effectively support professionals in their work, you may also want to implement your own program for self-care. There are many ways to do this, including the use of personal retreats in which you allocate time and space for utilization of the strategies that work best for you (Louden, 1997). The following list of self-care strategies has been generated over the years by students in my classes, whose ages span from 23-56, who come from a variety of ethnic, cultural, and racial backgrounds, who are both male and female, and who practice in a diverse array of settings. They have identified the following strategies:

- Spend more time with friends and family
- Enjoy evenings full of laughter, ice cream, and good times
- Exercise regularly
- Eat healthy food
- Take a bubble bath
- Paint
- Go to the beach
- Play in the water with children until your hands look like prunes
- Watch a sunset
- Read for leisure
- Take pleasure in life outside of work
- Gardening
- Kayaking or canoeing
- Snowmobiling
- Keep up on the latest news and research findings
- Hug someone
- Listen to music (singing along with the radio in the car works wonders)
- See movies (save the heavy dramas for when life isn't already full of drama)
- Talk to a friend
- Go for a walk
- Dance
- Get a good night's sleep every night
- Eat one piece of chocolate
- Reduce clutter
- Get more organized so that the details of everyday life don't add to stress
- Take a weekend retreat
- Yoga (active relaxation)
- Tai chi
- Take a vacation
- Take a day trip
- Listen to soft music in combination with deep breathing exercises
- Listen to a guided imagery tape
- Meditate
- Take at least 1-2 hours every week to do something you want to do
- Bicycling
- Hiking

- Take a ride in the car
- Have lunch with co-workers
- Go out to a nice restaurant with a friend
- Go shopping for yourself
- Avoid junk food
- Take time for appreciating or creating art
- Write in a journal
- Attend psychotherapy
- Recognize what triggers negative stress and avoid it
- Spend time with people who know you well enough to challenge you
- Snuggle with a pet
- Laugh loudly
- Commune with nature
- Get a massage
- Begin the day with gratitude and continue to practice it throughout the day
- Practice mindfulness
- Pray

As discussed in Chapter 7, many grief therapists also recommend the use of rituals in coping with grief. Rando (1984) notes that rituals of mourning can be very helpful to those who have experienced a loss. She underscores the importance of a ritual being personally meaningful if it is to have therapeutic value, with each individual defining for themselves what that means. Professional caregivers may find it helpful to create or participate in rituals that can assist with your own grief reactions. Worden (2002) states:

> A counselor can avoid burn-out by practicing active grieving. When a patient dies, it is important for a counselor to go through this period of active grieving. One thing I find personally helpful and recommend to our staff is that they attend the funeral services of the person with whom they have been working. It is also important that they allow themselves to experience the sadness and other feelings after someone dies, and not feel guilty if they do not grieve the same way for each death (p. 178).

I have participated in many discussions among professional caregivers about the benefits and drawbacks of attending funerals of clients/students or the family members of clients/students. Some professionals have reported that they attend based on the degree of involvement they have had with a client. Many health care and hospice workers have told me that attending the funeral for a patient they developed an attachment to has helped them with their own grief. Counselors in health and mental health organizations have noted that in work settings that do not allow time or space for personal grieving, attending the funeral of a patient or client can provide a place and time to reflect upon and grieve the loss. Others have noted that they view it as an opportunity to pay tribute to the individual or the family, which is part of their personal way of making meaning of loss.

As discussed previously, professionals need to make decisions about attending funerals or memorial services based on the therapeutic meaning to the client, whose possible need for privacy must be considered before the professional's personal needs. It is also important to reflect on and respect one's own limits and to practice multiple self-care strategies when doing this work. Therefore we must give ourselves permission not to attend a funeral or memorial service when we are feeling overloaded or stressed by obligations. Consulting a colleague or supervisor may be useful in helping you to make decisions about attending funerals. Many organizations find ways to support clients and staff in their grief through an annual memorial service that honors all clients or patients who have died. These provide an opportunity for co-workers to gather together and acknowledge the grief that results from work-related losses. Organizing such an event, or developing one's own personal grief rituals—such as listening to music that evokes feelings or lighting a candle in memory of significant relationships—may be useful to you in your future work.

Whether you make use of rituals or other methods of self-care, taking time regularly to identify strategies or resources you can use will help you to maintain your own sense of balance and well-being. If we are self-aware, understand how our own beliefs and feelings are affecting us, and practice self-care, we are better able to be empathic with someone else, wherever they are in the process of adjustment to loss.

Professional Support Systems

Seeking help for ourselves

At times, our work will trigger unresolved loss in our own lives, or secondary trauma may be more than we can manage with our usual coping strategies. There are times when we may observe ourselves, or others, using maladaptive strategies such as overworking, avoiding others, using substances, or shutting down our emotions in an effort to cope with powerful feelings or increased stress. If we observe these warning signs it is time to seek help.

> Never fall into the trap of believing that there is nothing you can do about the stress in your life. This stance quickly leads to passive or minimal coping efforts, demoralization, and increasing stress. An extreme instance of passive coping is the alcohol or drug abuse of the impaired caregiver (Larson, 1993, p.80).

Psychotherapy, pastoral counseling, grief or spiritual retreats led by experts, and/or treatment programs are not strategies of last resort, or exclusively for others. They can be the lifelines that enable us, just as they enable those we work with, to carry out the essential process of grief and find ways to cope most effectively. This is underscored by two experts in grief and loss, Maggie Callanan and Patricia Kelley (1992). They are hospice nurses who co-authored the book *Final Gifts: Understanding the Special Awareness, Needs, and Communications of the Dying.* They note:

Dealing with dying is hard work—physically and mentally—and it's very easy to slip into a frantic outlook that leaves you emotionally depleted, physically exhausted, and utterly overwhelmed. You'll do a better job if you take care of yourself. Let others share the burdens and responsibilities as well as the small victories and large sadnesses. Get plenty of rest. Eat well. Exercise regularly. Spend some time each day doing whatever relaxes you. It is important to get out of the house on a regular basis for something other than chores. Go to a movie, concert, or play. Enjoy eating out with a supportive friend. Consider attending meetings of support groups for others in your situation. Try relaxation techniques—music, meditation, imagery, prayer. Seek counseling if needed. After conducting a personal inventory, look around you. Will you reach out to others for the help you may need? (p. 212).

There are many options to choose from when we seek help for ourselves. Some of the same organizations and resources listed in previous chapters that provide assistance to grieving individuals may be able to help you, as a professional. Some of the same methods of individual or group counseling may be useful. A trusted supervisor or colleague may be able to refer you to an appropriate source of help.

Effective models of professional development and support have also been developed by organizations that regularly deal with grief and loss. Retreats for professionals coping with grief and loss may be built into a professional conference or a work-based staff development program. A sample agenda for this kind of retreat is included in the appendixes and is based on retreats I have facilitated regularly for hospice staff. Additional resources and planning aids for retreats are included in the books *20-Minute Retreats: Revive Your Spirit In Just Minutes a Day with Simple Self-Led Practices* (Harris, 2000), and *The Woman's Retreat Book: A Guide To Restoring, Rediscovering, and Reawakening Your True Self in a Moment, an Hour, a Day, or a Weekend* (Louden, 1997). These references include music suggestions, activities for creative expression, and rituals that serve as useful methods for both personal and professional respite, renewal, and inspiration.

Larson (1993) emphasizes that individuals as well as organizations need to take a proactive role in preventing burnout and managing stress related to professional caregiving. He notes that it is important to be proactive and that stress management "begins upstream":

There is a contemporary fable of a man who is walking beside a river and notices that someone is drowning. He jumps in, pulls the person to shore and revives him. Then another drowning person calls for help, and again the man successfully rescues him. As the man is about to walk away, a passerby shouts, 'Hey, there's another person drowning out there! Where are you going?' The man replies, 'I'm going upstream to see who's throwing all these people in!'

Much of our helping is downstream, rather than upstream, work. . . . As caregivers, it is helpful—both to us and to the people we assist—to look for any upstream interventions we can make. . . . These kinds of interventions can prevent some of the difficulties we repeatedly encounter downstream in helping (p. 79, 80).

It is my hope that the information included in this text will help you to accurately identify the many types of grief and loss reactions that you will encounter in your rewarding career as a professional helper. The text has also been designed to prepare you to develop intervention strategies that assist your clients, students, and yourself in coping with the loss and grief that inevitably occur with life's changes and challenges. Callanan and Kelley (1992), in the preface of *Final Gifts* write:

> We are not researchers or philosophers; we're nurses who choose to work with dying people. The material in this book has come directly from our finest teachers—our dying patients who have taught us what dying is like for them while they are experiencing it. What we have learned is so exciting and positive that it has changed our lives, and we have written this book to share those messages with you (p. 18).

Similarly, the material in this text has come directly from my finest teachers—the clients and families who were willing to share their lives and experiences with me as well as the extraordinarily committed students and colleagues who have contributed to my own learning. In her text, *After the Darkest Hour: How Suffering Begins the Journey To Wisdom,* psychotherapist Kathleen Brehony (2001) writes, "Why is it that some people can survive, even thrive, after the death of a loved one, or the diagnosis of a life-threatening illness, a job loss, or divorce?" Brehony also states, in an interview in the *Washington Post* with Barbara Mathias-Reigel (2002), "Suffering is usually the key that opens the door to a full realization of what we were born to do and the urge to embrace it."

While carrying out the essential work of helping those who are vulnerable, we all encounter suffering. While you may not have experienced the urge to embrace it, you clearly have chosen work that will open doors for yourself as well as for others. I think it is helpful to end this text with the same inspirational quote included in the beginning, thus coming full circle with the recognition that in order to help others with grief and loss we must also be aware of, and willing to deal with, our own.

> *Grief knits two hearts in closer bonds than happiness ever can; and common sufferings are far stronger links than common joys.*
>
> —Alphone de Lamartine

Exercise: Self-Evaluation

This is another exercise that students in a loss and grief course have found useful. It begins with some additional self-examination.

First, ask yourself the following questions:

1. Why am I drawn to the work I do?
2. Now that you have studied the information in this text on loss and grief, what feelings are you aware of as you think about more in-depth work with others experiencing grief?

3. What are some of the professional development methods and organizational resources you have learned about that you believe have usefulness in facilitating the effective functioning of professional caregivers?
4. What plans do you have to sustain yourself in your work with grieving clients in the future? What strategies and methods do you plan to use personally to prevent burn-out and compassion fatigue, and to maintain a balance in your personal and professional life?

Self-Test

1. When is compassion fatigue likely to occur?
   a. When one faces more than three losses in close proximity
   b. When a caregiver has worked a 24-hour shift
   c. When a caregiver is providing care to a grieving community
   d. When an imbalance occurs between self-care and caring for others

2. Which of the following is considered a maladaptive coping response to the stress of being a professional caregiver?
   a. Grieving
   b. Attending funerals of clients
   c. Overworking
   d. Writing or talking frequently about loss

Answers: 1) d   2) c

Internet Resources

Resources to aid the helping professional in coping with grief can be found at http://www. journeyofhearts.org/jofh/grief/cope
Founded by a grief therapist, the Center for Loss site offers a variety of professional training workshops on grief and loss at http://www.centerforloss.com
Relax-online provides relaxation and guided imagery exercises to relieve stress at http://www. relax-online.com/imageryonline.htm
Nurses can choose from a wide array of professional development, networking, and continuing education opportunities. Examples include offerings through the Oncology Nursing Society at http://www.ons.org and the American Nurses Association at http://nursingworld. org
The Association of Oncology Social Work is just one of many professional organizations offering continuing education through distance learning courses in end of life care and annual professional conferences. http://www.aosw.org

References

Brehony, K. (2001). *After the darkest hour: How suffering begins the journey to wisdom.* New York: Owl Books.
Callanan, M., & Kelley, P. (1992). *Final gifts: Understanding the special awareness, needs and communications of the dying.* New York: Poseidon Press.

Cskai, E., & Walsh-Burke, K. (2005). Social work education and training in end of life and palliative care. *Journal of Social Work in End of Life and Palliative Care,* Vol. 2, in press.

Durfee, M. (2004). *Facing the issues: Grief and mourning.* International Child Abuse Network. Retrieved January, 25, 2004 from http://66.127.183.74/articles/grmourn.html

Harris, R. (2000). *20-minute retreats: Revive your spirit in just minutes a day with simple self-led practices.* New York: Owl Press.

Larson, D. G. (1993). *The helper's journey: Working with people facing grief, loss, and life-threatening illness.* Champaign, IL: Research Press Company.

Louden, J. (1997). *The woman's retreat book: A guide to restoring, rediscovering, and reawakening your true self in a moment, an hour, a day, or a weekend.* San Francisco: Harper Collins.

Mathias-Reigel, B. (2002). *Coping with unpredictable changes in life.* Retrieved February 25, 2002 from http://washingtonpost.com/wp-dyn/articles/A54919-2001Feb25.html

Pfifferling, J., & Gilley, K. (2000). Overcoming compassion fatigue. *Family Practice Management,* April. Retrieved January 27, 2004 from http://www.aafp.org/fpm/20000400/39over.html

Rando, T. (1984). *Grief, dying, and death: Clinical interventions for caregivers.* Champaign, IL: Research Press Company.

Worden, W. (2002). *Grief counseling and grief therapy: A handbook for the mental health practitioner.* (3rd ed.). New York: Springer Publishing.

Appendix A

Common Losses Across the Lifespan

Childhood	Adolescence	Young Adulthood	Middle Adulthood	Later Adulthood
Death of parent	Any of the losses listed in childhood	Any of the losses listed in childhood and adolescence	Any of the losses listed in childhood, adolescence, and young adulthood	Any of the losses listed in childhood, adolescence, young and middle adulthood
Separation from parent or primary caregiver	Loss of significant relationships	Loss of partner	Loss of work/career	Loss of support network
Death of grandparent	Loss of connection to spiritual community	Loss of job	Loss of health	Loss of mobility
Death of pet		Loss of income	Launching of children/ change in role as parent	Retirement/ loss of career
Loss of two-parent family	Loss of earlier identities	Loss of sobriety		
Moving from/loss of familiar home	Loss of self-efficacy	Loss of faith	Death of child	Loss of memory
Loss of teachers, counselors		Incarceration/ loss of freedom	Loss of vision, hearing	Loss of independence
Loss of friends			Loss of libido	
Loss of innocence				
Loss of sense of omnipotence				

This table is based on several theories including life-span and attachment theories. While not every loss listed is *perceived* as a loss by individuals who experience them, and individuals in earlier stages of life may experience losses that are more common at later stages, these are some of the common experiences that may engender grief reactions.

Additional Resources

Bridges, W. (1980). *Transitions: Making sense of life's changes.* New York: Addison-Wesley Publishing Co.

Holmes, T.H., & Rahe, R.H. (1967). The social readjustment rating scale. *Journal of Psychosomatic Research, 11*(2), 213-218.

Mannino, J. D. (1997). *Grieving days, healing days.* Needham Heights, MA: Allyn & Bacon.

Viorst, J. (1998). *Necessary losses: The loves, illusions, dependencies, and impossible expectations that all of us have to give up in order to grow.* New York: The Free Press.

Appendix B

Annotated Bibliography

For Preschool Aged Children

Brown, Margaret Wise. (1958) *The dead bird*. Reading, MA: Addison-Wesley. In simple words and pictures this book helps children understand the reactions of a group of children to the death of a bird. (Fiction)

De Paola, Tommie. (1973) *Nana upstairs and Nana downstairs*. New York: Putnam. This story describes the death of a great-grandmother (Nana Upstairs) while grandmother (Nana Downstairs) and her grandson go on to remember her. (Fiction)

Grollman, Earl. (1990). *Talking about death: A dialogue between parent and child*. This book may be helpful to families with children of different ages who are coping with death. In simple language with pictures, it provides the framework for parents and children to discuss the topic of death. (Non-fiction)

Stein, Sara. (1974). *About dying: An open family book for parents and children*. New York: Walker Books. This read-aloud book with pictures helps parents explain death to young children. (Non-fiction)

Viorst, Judith. (1971). *The tenth good thing about Barney*. New York: Atheneum Publications. After Barney, a beloved pet, dies, he is remembered for the good things about him while he lived and for helping flowers to grow where his body is buried. (Fiction)

Zolotow, Charlotte. (1974). *My grandson Lew*. New York: Harper & Row. In this book a young boy recalls his grandfather and learns to cope with his loss. (Fiction)

For Elementary School Aged Children

Alcott, Louisa M. (1969). *Little women*. New York: Macmillan. This timeless classic has provided many children with their first exposure to the death of a sibling. (Fiction)

Buscaglia, Leo. (1982). *The fall of Freddie the leaf*. New Jersey: Holt, Reinhart & Winston. In words and pictures this book addresses death as a part of the life of Freddie, a leaf, and his friends. (Fiction)

Clifton, Lucille. (1983). *Everett Anderson's goodbye*. New York: Henry Holt & Company. One of the few books with pictures depicting an African American boy whose father has died. This inspirational story of hope is a Coretta Scott King Award winner. (Fiction)

Coburn, John. (1964). *Anne and the sand dobbies*. New York: Seabury Press. A young boy learns what it means to die through the help of a friend and his imaginary sand dobbies. (Fiction)

Krasny Brown, Lavrie (1998). *When dinosaurs die*. Boston: Little, Brown & Company. This book receives high praise from many helping professionals. (Fiction)

Krementz, Jill. (1981). *How it feels when a parent dies*. New York: Alfred A. Knopf. Many grieving children of different ages have found this book very helpful. Children and teens from ages 7 to 18 share their personal experiences with the death of a parent and how they have coped. Photographs help to provide a sense of familiarity. (Non-fiction)

Mann, Peggy. (1977). *There are two kinds of terrible*. New York: Doubleday. After his mother dies, a young boy learns to cope with the loss, as well as with the difficulties of his grieving father. (Fiction)

Martin, Ann M. (1986). *With you and without you*. New York: Scholastic, Inc. This book, by the author of the popular Babysitters Club books, is about the illness and death of Liza O'Hara's father and how her family copes with the loss. (Fiction)

Patterson, Katherine. (1977). *Bridge to Terabithia*. New York: Corwell. An award-winning story of the close friendship of a boy and girl and the impact of her death. (Fiction)

Richter, Elizabeth. (1986). *Losing someone you love: When a brother or sister dies*. New York: Putnam. Children share their own experiences about the death of a brother or sister. (Non-fiction)

Thomas, Jane R. (1988). *Saying goodbye to grandma*. New York: Clarion Books. A young girl describes her family's experience attending the funeral of her grandmother. (Fiction)

White, E.B. (1952). *Charlotte's web*. New York: Harper & Row. Another classic about the life and death of a spider, Charlotte, with a hopeful ending about life continuing for survivors after a loss. (Fiction)

Williams, Margery. (1971). *The velveteen rabbit*. Garden City, NY: Doubleday. A beautifully written classic about serious illness and the meaning of life from a toy rabbit's perspective. (Fiction)

For Pre-Adolescents and Adolescents

Agee, James. (1959). *A death in the family*. New York: Avon. A classic which is sensitively written about how a family copes with the loss of their father. (Fiction)

Blume, Judy. (1981). *Tiger eyes*. New York: Dell. Fictitious story by a popular author about a girl who must cope with her father's murder. (Fiction)

Crane, Stephen. (1951). *Red badge of courage*. New York: Random House. Another classic which deals with death from war through the personal reactions of a young Civil War soldier. (Fiction)

Frank, Anne. (1963). *The diary of a young girl*. New York: Washington Square Press. The autobiography of a teenaged Jewish girl in hiding during the Holocaust. (Non-fiction)

Grollman, Earl. (1993). *Straight talk about death for teenagers: How to cope with losing someone you love*. Boston: Beacon Press. This book is written for teenagers and acknowledges the importance of their experiences of grief while addressing common feelings and how to cope with them. (Non-fiction)

Klein, Norma. (1974). *Sunshine*. New York: Avon. The life story of a nineteen-year-old girl who dies, based on her diary and tapes. (Non-fiction)

LeShan, Eda. (1976). *Learning to say goodbye.* New York: Macmillan. This is a very helpful resource written for adolescents about the experience of losing a parent to death. (Non-fiction)

Rofes, Eric. (1985). *The kid's book about death and dying.* Boston: Little, Brown & Company. Eleven- to 14-year-olds share their experiences with death. Written for teens by teens. (Non-fiction)

Schotter, Roni. (1979). *A matter of time.* New York: Philomel. A sixteen-year-old girl's mother dies and she is helped through the painful experience by a social worker. Helpful for teens referred to counseling. (Fiction)

Books for Adult Caregivers

Fitzgerald, Helen. (1992). *The grieving child: A parent's guide.* New York: Simon and Schuster.

Gaffney, Donna. (1988). *The seasons of grief: Helping your children grow through their loss.* New York: New American Library.

Grollman, Earl. (1967). *Explaining death to children.* Boston: Beacon Press.

Grollman, Earl. (1974). *Concerning death: A practical guide to the living.* Boston: Beacon Press.

Kubler-Ross, Elizabeth. (1983). *On children and death.* New York: Macmillan.

Rando, Therese. (1991). *How to go on living when someone you love has died.* New York: Bantam Books.

Stillman, Peter. (1990). *Answers to a child's questions about death.* Stamford, NY: Guidelines Publications.

Wells, Rosemary. (1992). *Helping children cope with grief—facing death in the family.* London: Sheldon Press.

Books for Grieving Adults

DiGiulio, Robert. (1988). *Beyond widowhood.* New York: The Free Press.

Grollman, Earl. (1974). *Concerning death: A practical guide to the living.* Boston: Beacon Press.

Grollman, Earl. (1987). *Time remembered: A journal for survivors.* Boston: Beacon Press.

Kreis, Bernadine & Alice Pattie. (1982). *Up from grief: Patterns of recovery.* New York: Seabury Press.

Kushner, Harold. (1981). *When bad things happen to good people.* New York: Schocken Books.

Lerner, Gerda. (1978). *A death of one's own.* New York: Harper & Row.

Rando, Therese. (1993). *How to go on living when someone you love dies.* New York: Bantam Books.

Appendix C

Helpful Strategies for Coping with Grief

As a bereavement counselor and social worker, I have worked closely with many families and communities affected by loss. What I have found through my twenty years of experience is that many people feel confused or unsure about how to cope with their own grief or the grief of others. Not knowing what to do or say, people often mistakenly avoid talking about or dealing with grief altogether. Unfortunately, this can lead to further misunderstanding and leave people who need to be connected feeling isolated and alone. The following strategies can help you and those you care about through the grief process.

Acknowledge the loss.

Time alone does not heal. It is what people do over time that matters. To facilitate healing, people need to be able to acknowledge their loss, express their feelings, and feel a sense of connection with the person who has died as well as to those in their support group who are still living.

Express and share feelings.

The period following a loss is a very sad and vulnerable time for people who are grieving. Yet many people coping with grief have expressed that even though it can be painful at times, they also find it comforting to have opportunities to express and share their feelings in a safe and nurturing environment. This connection provides a source of comfort and strength, thereby creating a foundation for healing to begin.

Encourage sharing and offer to listen.

We sometimes feel that tears or other expressions of feelings are signs of weakness or a reflection that we are not handling things well. However, these expressions are a normal and healthy response to loss. Friends and family can help by being supportive listeners and by encouraging survivors, when they feel ready, to share these heartfelt emotions.

Allow for differences in the needs of grieving people.

There is no designated timeline for how long the grieving process should last. There are no "shoulds" with grieving. It is important that people process and work through their grief in a way that feels comfortable to them.

Share memories of loved ones to help in healing.

Healing comes not from forgetting, but from remembering those who have died and the special times that were shared. One way to do this is by creating a special ritual of remembrance, such as candle lighting, to honor and remember loved ones. Lighting the candle during times of personal reflection or at gatherings with family and friends can help to create a sense of peace and keep the memories of loved ones alive in our hearts.

Appendix D

Strategies for Professionals Helping Children and Families Cope with Traumatic Loss

In assisting families, organizations, or communities during or following traumatic events, keep in mind that:

1. **Natural human reactions to tragedy** range from:
    *   Anger to rage
    *   Anxiety to terror
    *   Sadness to intense grief
    *   Relief to guilt
    *   Despair to hope

2. These natural **feelings need to be acknowledged** and support offered. Sometimes just listening can be most helpful.

3. Children's, teens', and adults' **reactions will be partly influenced by their previous experiences** with trauma and loss.

4. **Children will understand and react differently**, depending on their stage of emotional and cognitive development. Information and support should be tailored to their developmental needs.

5. **Feelings of increased vulnerability** need to be acknowledged and reassurance provided.

6. **Reassurance should be provided** through statements such as, "Adults in authority are working very hard to be sure that everyone in our family and our communities will be safe and secure."

7. Families, groups, and communities **gain support and strength through gathering together** and acknowledging and expressing feelings of loss as well as hope. Helping people cope through such a gathering is important.

8. Parents and professionals can help families **establish plans and methods to be in touch with each other in the days and weeks following the trauma** to provide reassurance and support.

9. **Sharing memories** of those we have loved and lost helps with healing.

Appendix E

Remembrance Celebrations: Planning Your Own Memorial Service

That which is important can only be felt with the heart.

—Helen Keller

Life is no brief candle to me. It is a sort of splendid torch which I have got hold of for the moment, and I want to make it burn as brightly as possible before handing it on to future generations.

—George Bernard Shaw

The inspiration for including this set of suggestions has come from many sources—mainly from the people I have known who have extended to me the privilege of knowing them, their sorrows and their joys, their accomplishments, and the meaning they have made from life. In my role as a social worker I have come to know hundreds of people who have let me share in their lives and the lives of their loved ones. One individual, in particular, had an extraordinary influence on me.

Lisa was 46, the mother of three teenagers, and a spirited mother, daughter, sister, and wife. Together with her husband, she had accumulated a close circle of friends, was active in her synagogue, and was a highly respected and valued community member. Although we lived in the same community, I didn't meet her until she experienced a recurrence of cancer and called me for counseling. She explained that she was the sort of person who prided herself on tackling problems head-on. While she had received life-extending treatment after her initial diagnosis and was making every effort to continue living, she was also determined to plan for the possibility that her life might be shortened. She wanted to be sure her family's needs were met, whether she survived or died. She therefore began to give some of her energy to reviewing her life and legacy with her family, friends, and the important people in her life. She held a celebratory gathering in her home while she was still able to celebrate a lifetime of memories and meaningful relationships. And while most people will not choose this type of memorial, the same activities and procedures can be very useful to include in a traditional (or non-traditional) memorial ceremony.

We live in a time and a place in which the occasions that mark beginnings—births, bat mitzvahs, marriages, graduations—are celebrated with rituals and ceremonies and free expression of feelings. We plan our celebrations with great care, being sure to include important people, providing food we know they will enjoy, and often incorporating music, toasts, and acknowledgment of the importance of relationships in our lives. Often we begin this planning process years in advance of the event; we imagine what we will say, who we will include and what our invitations will look like. Yet, when it comes to one of the most meaningful celebrations of our lives, very few of us plan our own funerals or memorial services. The lists below include resources that can be helpful to individuals, families, and friends anticipating or planning a funeral or memorial service.

Information Prior to Death Concerning Preferences

> Organ Donation
> Advance Directives
> Health Care Proxy Designated
> Preferred Funerary or Memorial Plan
> Spiritual Connections or Practices

Information After Death

> Personal Biographical Information (Often included in the obituary)
> Funeral Information (Where and when it will take place)
> Notification Checklist (Who should be contacted and informed of the death)

For the Memorial/Funeral Service/Ritual

Program Designs
A small pamphlet or brochure to guide participants through the service is very helpful. It may include a listing with the following information:

- What will take place during the service
- Who will lead the service/memorial
- Who else will speak or participate
- Musical selections
- Poetry or inspirations
- Pictures, artwork, or mementos
- Activities in which all can participate (for example, visiting the cemetery following the service, placing flowers in a memorial vase, signing a guest book)

Quotations

A list of inspirations can be found at http://www.comfortcandles.com under the Inspirations link. The references listed below also include inspirations and quotations.

Helpful Organizations and Web Sites _____

http://www.aarp.org   The American Association of Retired People's site with Web links and advance directives information.

http://www.beyondindigo.com   Funeral planning forms, information on grief and terminal illness.

http://www.agingwithdignity.org/5wishes.html   The five wishes document for advance planning is very helpful.

http://www.aarp.org/bulletin/consumer/Articles/a2003-06-30-funeralplanning.html   The American Association of Retired People's Web site for funeral planning resources.

http.//www.abcd-caring.org/resources.htm   Americans for Better Care of the Dying resources for advance directives and end of life decision-making.

http://www.partnershipforcaring.org/HomePage/   Advance directives link gives state-by-state information on advance care planning.

http://www.partnershipforcaring.org/ToolKits/family_set.html   Resources for funeral and memorial service planning.

Helpful References _____

Bennett, A., & Foley, B. (1997). *In memoriam: A practical guide to planning a memorial service*. New York: Fireside Books.

Doan, E.C. (1989). *Speaker's sourcebook II*. Grand Rapids, MI: Zondervan.

Sublette, K., & Flagg, M. (1992). *Final celebrations: A guide for personal and family funeral planning*. Ventura, CA: Pathfinder Publishing of California.

Lynn, J., & Harrold, J. (1999). *Handbook for mortals: Guidance for people facing serious illness*. New York: Oxford Press.

Appendix F

Expressive Techniques

Many people, professionals and non-professionals alike, find it very helpful to express their thoughts and feelings through the arts, writing, and other vehicles of communication. This can especially be true when the feelings and thoughts are powerful, such as those connected to grief and loss. Below are just a few of the expressive techniques clients and colleagues have shared with me. There are two examples included as well. The first is a poem by Ernestine Mason, written while she processed her feelings related to death that arose during her study of the topic of loss and bereavement. The second is a "letter" written by my 8-year-old daughter Jessy, to her cousin Haley, after Haley's death from Sudden Infant Death Syndrome. They are illustrative of the therapeutic value of creative expression and I am grateful to Ernestine and Jessy for sharing them.

Writing

Keeping a journal, writing poetry, and participating in writing workshops can be helpful in coping with grief and loss. These activities can be carried out independently or included in bereavement support groups, classes on loss and grief, and school assignments.

Art Activities

Many people of all ages have given expression to their feelings through painting, drawing, and other artistic mediums. In our children's bereavement groups, we have used activities such as making memorial boxes in which to store mementos; creating memory books; making candles and lighting them in a memorial closing ceremony; and making picture frames in which to keep the picture of a loved one, a family home from which one has moved, or other important reminders. Chapter 7 described a boat ceremony held at a family camp program for families who have accumulated many losses from AIDS and HIV. Similar activities are often used in bereavement camps and retreats.

Dance and the Performing Arts

Physical forms of expression are easier for some individuals and groups than verbal expressions. Physical activities such as focused breathing exercises, used often in conjunction with guided imagery, can be helpful, especially when feelings are very powerful.

You may find some helpful suggestions for activities in Angela Hobday and Kate Ollier's (1999) book, *Creative Therapy with Children and Adolescents*. (Impact Publishers, Inc.). Useful exercises can be found in the workbook by Marge Heegaard (1991) entitled *When Something Terrible Happens: Children Can Learn to Cope with Grief*. (Woodland Press).

The Wind in My Sails

I sail along, looking in the far distance,
where the blue sea appears to be touching the blue skies.
Deceptive illusions, things are not always as they seem.
Sailing reminds me so much of life.

The wind is crucial to sailing. I simply adjust my sails to
Court the winds, to stay on course. This suits me as
I feel the warmth of the sun, the rhythmic beat of the
Waves against the boat and the smell of the ocean.

There were times when I encountered stormy waters.
Choppy waters. Waters, angrier than myself.
I rode the waves, knowing that going with the flow, as if
I had a choice, was my best recourse.
This will not be the last time I drift astray; life is full of risks.
I say a prayer, in my mind and aloud.
God, keep me safe and the wind in my sails.
Sailing challenges my faith.

My compass keeps me going in the right direction, or so it seems.
North, northeast, south, southwest. East. West.
No matter how far out I sail, I return with a different
Perspective of my strengths, my vulnerabilities and life.
Sailing keeps me anchored.

The further out I sail increases my feelings of trepidation,
But I continue, in spite of myself because I know I can not sail
In shallow water. As I recheck my life jacket, I pray for favorable winds.
God, please keep the wind at my back.
If water is symbolic for life, I am being born again and again.

Each sail presents unique challenges. What will I encounter this time? My memories
comfort me as I think of other excursions out to sea.

My ship has come in. Anchored. Docked. No more sailing, or so it seems.
As I drift back and forth into other realms of reality, I ask God to keep the wind in my
sails, as I greet whatever awaits my soul. Old sailors never die.

Ernestine Mason

Appendix G

Caregiver's Retreat Agenda
and Invitation

Staff retreats or team development meetings can help to sustain hope and competence in professionals who frequently encounter grief. The sample agenda and invitation included here are examples of what can be sent to participants in advance of the retreat so they can come prepared.

Sample Agenda

9:00 a.m. Welcome and refreshments

As people gather together each of the participants is asked to think about and respond to the following scenario:

The day is over. You're returning home, or have just returned to work. A trusted person (partner, friend, colleague) asks, "How was the team development session?" You respond, "It was one of the best sessions we could have had!" What would have happened during this day that would lead you to say this? Be as specific as possible!

Next, ask people to identify what items of significance they may have brought or thought about that help sustain them in their work. (As noted in the pre-retreat invitation, a thank you letter, memento from a client or student, a picture, or a piece of music might be identified.) Participants can be invited to share their items just before or after each activity break in the day.

10:00 a.m. Icebreaker—getting acquainted exercise

Example: *Something in my pocket(book)*. In this activity, each participant is asked to find three items in their pocket or pocketbook that signify something about them and share the items with the group. (This provides information about multiple aspects of workers' lives and helps people get acquainted with what they have in common as well as unique differences.)

10:30 a.m. What brings you to this work?

Each participant is asked to share with the group what led them to working in their field and why they are interested in the topic of the retreat.

11:00 a.m. A window into feelings about our work

Each participant is given a piece of paper and asked to draw four squares. Then they are asked to complete each square with a picture or a description in words of the following:

A loss that has been significant for you.	An event that has occurred in your work that has significance for you.
A personal goal for your future.	Something you feel individually proud of regarding the work you've done with clients.

Each participant is then asked to share two of the items they have written or drawn. If the group is large, it can be divided into smaller groups or pairs. The facilitator helps the group recap or summarize some of the key descriptions that were shared, noting common themes and unique experiences or expressions.

11:30 a.m. Providing positive feedback

Team members can be asked to identify strengths or contributions they have witnessed in other team members that make their work more manageable. This is very helpful for interdisciplinary or multidisciplinary teams who may not always articulate to each other what they appreciate.

12:00 p.m. Lunch

It is helpful to provide nutritious food that conveys caring and comfort. Music that creates an atmosphere of light and serenity is also helpful.

1:00 p.m. Sharing stories

Participants can be asked, if they have not done so already, to share items of significance they brought or that they keep in their offices, homes, or hearts. These items are often connected to powerful stories related to loss and hope from which all participants can gain understanding. Facilitators should be prepared to share a story, piece of music, or item of significance as well.

2:00 p.m. Writing exercise

The facilitator presents a box of random items (masking tape, Band-Aids, earplugs, candles, chocolates, sacred books) that may serve as metaphors for the experiences of professional caregivers. Each participant is asked to choose one and write about how the item symbolizes what they experience in their work. Music can be played while participants write for approximately 15 minutes. They can be encouraged to write a poem, essay, or in any form they choose. Participants are encouraged to share their work if they wish. Only positive feedback about the writing style or content is encouraged.

3:00 p.m. Generating homework

Participants are each given a blank piece of stationary and an envelope and asked to write their hopes and goals for their future work. They will be asked to seal the letter and put it in a safe place, to be opened one or two years later as a reminder of the work they did during the retreat.

3:45 p.m. Appreciation

Each participant puts their name on a colorful piece of paper and places it on their chair. All participants are then given a colored pen or pencil. Each participant then moves around the room, writing a personalized positive statement of appreciation for every participant. Everyone is then asked to read their sheets silently. Then, in order to acknowledge the appreciation they received, each participant reads aloud to the group one or two of the statements written about them.

4:30 p.m. Closing Exercise: A Rose, a Thorn, and a Bud

With the participants gathered in a circle, the leader asks each person to think about the experience they have had together and to think about sharing "a rose, a bud, and a thorn." The rose represents a positive experience, the thorn represents something that caused discomfort or impeded enjoyment, and the bud represents a new idea to be used in the future.

Sample Invitation

[Date]

Dear Hospice Team Members,

I am very much looking forward to our team retreat on [date]. I have read your suggestions for topics you would like to explore in our time together and appreciate your taking the time to do this.

In the time we spend together we will be working on team-building and communication activities that will draw on the many strengths and different abilities of team members, so please dress comfortably. Sneakers or comfortable shoes, and slacks or shorts will work well. In addition, please think about and bring with you an item that is a reminder of why you do the important work for hospice that you do. The item might be a thank you note from a family, an inspirational poem, an article from a professional journal or book chapter that you used in your training, or a piece of music you like. The item should be representative of what gives you a sense of purpose or motivation in your work. Please bring this item with you to the retreat. This portion will constitute Session I, with a follow up later in the summer.

Again, I am very much looking forward to working with you and thank you for making the commitment to your team in this way. I will see you soon.

Best Wishes,

[retreat leader]

Index